Homeless Not Hopeless

The Survival Networks of Latino and African American Men

Edna Molina-Jackson

UNIVERSITY PRESS OF AMERICA,® INC.
Lanham • Boulder • New York • Toronto • Plymouth, UK

**Copyright © 2008 by
University Press of America,® Inc.**
4501 Forbes Boulevard
Suite 200
Lanham, Maryland 20706
UPA Acquisitions Department (301) 459-3366

Estover Road
Plymouth PL6 7PY
United Kingdom

Library of Congress Control Number: 2008922692
ISBN-13: 978-0-7618-4045-9 (paperback : alk. paper)
ISBN-10: 0-7618-4045-1 (paperback : alk. paper)
eISBN-13: 978-0-7618-4167-8
eISBN-10: 0-7618-4167-9

∞™ The paper used in this publication meets the minimum
requirements of American National Standard for Information
Sciences—Permanence of Paper for Printed Library Materials,
ANSI Z39.48—1984

For my son Luke . . . when you've grown enough to read this book,
I hope its pages will reveal to you that compassion is not as much a
virtue as it is a simple yet profound realization
of our oneness as people.

And for all our brothers and sisters who continue to endure the
harsh reality of life without a home . . . your struggle is not
forgotten and certainly there is hope.

Contents

Preface

During an all-night census blitz to enumerate a segment of the homeless population that on any given night may sleep outdoors on the streets of Los Angeles's Skid Row area, I discovered what can happen to people that are very hard-pressed by socio-economic forces. It was many years ago, while working for the RAND Corporation on a large-scale homelessness study that accompanied by thirty-plus interviews and plain clothes policemen I surveyed miles of census-blocks in downtown Los Angeles's Skid Row and business district attempting to count "the homeless street population" dwelling in this region. Even today the images of that night remain indelibly recorded in my minds-eye. The nightly street rituals of people sleeping out on the streets of Skid Row resembled something out of a strange sci-fi movie where the moral commentary of the story bites hard against the dispassionate and cynical viewer's disbelief. What I saw on that census night most Americans would think is the lot of people living in less-developed nations whose political and economic resources are ill-equipped to handle massive poverty. However, the sight of thousands of people huddled together on the streets, sleeping in card board boxes, dirty blankets or layered newspapers, under stairways and freeway overpasses, in public parks, cars and abandoned building—illuminated by a barrage of small trash-can fires lit to defend against the inhospitable cold night—these images represent the very gripping reality replayed nightly in one of America's most prominent cities, Los Angeles. Although news media documentaries make visible the plight of homeless people in less-developed countries, I must admit that from the "economically safe" distance of life in U.S. society the harshness of such poverty was less palpable to me. I recall as a child traveling with my parents south from the United States to Mexico (along the San Diego-to-Tijuana border), and witnessing the unpleasant sight of Tijuana's hillsides shockingly landscaped with the numerous, make-shift houses of Mexico's poor and homeless. Still, I never expected to see people in the United States living under similar forms of economic despair.

Taken literally, homelessness is essentially a housing problem, that is, it results from a lack of access to conventional housing. Yet research indicates that homelessness also results from a variety of additional, long standing social problems affecting individuals that can range from social isolation, physical, mental and/or behavioral disabilities to persistent unemployment (Koegel, et. al. 1995; Snow and Anderson 1993; Rossi 1988). In the last two decades, homelessness researchers have examined these factors at length, attempting to deepen society's understanding of the complexity of homeless experiences found in America. Inadvertently, such efforts have also contributed to a reification of homelessness itself, which tends to obscure the fundamental aspect of this problem—that is, as a case of extreme poverty. This reification of homelessness further undermines efforts to generate corrective policy measures, given traditionally unsympathetic portraits of "the homeless" as marginal, transient members of society undeserving of expansive government support or services. As homelessness results from extreme poverty, extremely impoverished people find it difficult to secure the most essential resources and given the limited availability of low-income housing (especially in prominent states like California) the odds of obtaining permanent housing are stacked against them.

Fully twenty years have passed since homelessness first gained national attention as a major social problem in America. During the mid-1980s the situation of homelessness was recognized as a national crisis, shortly after the Reagan Administration implemented two important policy decisions that had adverse ramifications for many low-income people in the U.S. In one decision, the administration drastically cut the federal budget for domestic programs, funding decreased from $32 billion in 1981 to $6 billion by 1989, this in turn negatively impacted housing assistance programs nationwide (Appelbaum 1989). In another decision, the administration's policy of de-institutionalizing mentally ill patients prompted an increase in the estimated size of the homeless population by half a million nationwide (Coates, 1990). By the late 1980s, amid growing public concerns regarding the visibly increasing size of the homeless population, the U.S. Congress passed the Stewart B. McKinney Homeless Assistance Act in 1987 (Burt, et. al. 2001). The McKinney Act subsidized funding for state and local programs that provide assistance to homeless individuals (acting essentially as a type of federal *dollar-matching funding* for existing or newly developed programs). However under the Reagan administration the implementation of McKinney Act programs remained severely under-funded for several years (Burt, et. al. 2001).

From a poverty analyst perspective, the 1980s were a political era punctuated by funding cutbacks in subsistence and income maintenance programs which led to rising poverty rates, particularly among working families for whom poverty rates increased by 25% (Greenstein and Jaeger 1992), and by the escalating numbers of homeless people. This era was further underscored by a hardened socio-political climate that was fueled by the rhetoric of the deficiency-oriented theorists who claimed such undesirable outcomes were due to individual behavioral deficiencies that lead to extreme poverty. For example, in the late 1950s into the 1960s, Social Anthropologist Oscar Lewis was among the strongest proponent of this view of the poor and by the mid-1980s Charles Murray reinvigorated the argument in his book, Losing Ground. In 1994 Murray with his coauthor Herrnstein released yet another assault on the poor in their work entitled, The Bell Curve, in which they took their deficiency argument further by claiming a biological basis for the inferiority of the poor. By resorting essentially to a 'character assault" on the poor, political leaders during that time in effect absolved the government of any responsibility for the rising rates of poverty and homelessness, and instead claimed these problems were due to the deficiencies and vulnerabilities of the poor and homeless themselves. The unsympathetic climate of the 1980s toward the poor gained such momentum with the American public (not surprising, given the barrage of nightly news stories reporting on welfare fraud and abuse) that even the democrats followed their predecessors and signed into law the Welfare Reform Bill of 1996—which drastically cut aid to the poor (particularly, to woman and children who were once seen as most deserving of support). U.S. public policy which had once been a haven for the ". . . huddled masses yearning to breathe free" (Laxarus 1883), shifted from its universalistic view that entitled all people to minimal subsistence resources (basic needs such as food, housing, clothing), toward a more exceptionalist view of social justice that makes government aid provisional; that is, available only to those judged as deserving (Katz 1989).

It was in the midst of this backlash against the most financially hardpressed individuals in American society that homelessness researchers set out to redress the misinformation generated about the nature of extreme poverty experienced in America and to redirect the public's attention toward its political and economic causes; in short, to accurately inform Americans about the nature and causes of extreme poverty that lead to homelessness. To this end, twenty years of research were aimed at dispelling myths about the deficient character of homeless people (by presenting numerous accounts of their daily struggles to survive on the streets); at exemplifying the larger social structural constraints (political and economic policies) that operate to produce extreme poverty and its consequence, homelessness; and also at strongly advocating for corrective policy measures.

This book examines the roles that homeless people and the U.S. government play in causing and curtailing the escalating phenomena of homelessness. The analyses presented herein, provide 'a day in the life' examination of the experiences of homeless men, coupled with a secondary examination of the social structural impact of policies matters of on housing and poverty. Chapter 1 opens with a discussion of the social or personal networking framework used to examine the experiences of homelessness among Latino and African American men and presents demographic information on these participants as well. Chapter 2 provides an overview of the research on minority homelessness and further contextualizes African American and Latino populations in terms of demographic census data, issues shaping their integration into U.S. society and ends with a brief look at the social world of these homeless men. Chapter 3 provides a detailed examination of the informal non-kin networks that exist among homeless Latinos and African Americans and includes descriptions of the form and functioning of their respective networks. Chapter 4 discusses the saliency of even weak ties within the social networks of homeless men. Here it becomes clear that the range in levels of social intimacy in their relationships with acquaintances and associates can be instrumental in generating a variety of resources that make survival on the streets of Skid Row possible. In chapter 5, "Getting by with A Little Help from Their Friends," the focus shifts from network ties that involve low levels of social intimacy to those characterized by high social intimacy. It's important to note that each type of linkage (whether acquaintance, associate or friend) carries with it a host of expectations in terms of how such relationships function and the extent of reciprocity in resource exchange required for continued network participation (i.e., to protect against being dropped from the network and its resources). The book concludes, chapter 6, with a discussion of the issues homeless individuals confront in their plight to survive the experience of extreme poverty in America. Furthermore, the policy implications of the study are highlighted here as well. Among the policy implications discussed are the need to alter the socio-economic structures that generate extreme and entrenched forms of poverty that then lead to homelessness and the importance of going beyond containment-oriented policies and moving toward enacting a national policy to end homelessness.

Acknowledgments

I would like to end by acknowledging family, friends and colleagues that supported my efforts throughout the writing of this book. And given the model of family first practiced by many Latinos, I start by acknowledging *mi familia*. I am happily indebted to my wonderful son Luke and my life's companion and husband, Richard for the joy they bring to my life; together they are the silliest, most endearing and mischievous stewards of my heart! And during those times when I become overwhelmed by the suffering that exists in the world, Richard reminds me of the abundant nature of kindness and joy that await my embrace. Many thanks to my sister and brothers, *mis hermanos*, Javi, Mari and Paco (who is more than a brother-in-law . . . he has unquestionably become my *brother from another mother*) for their support and smiles which always arrive just when I need them most! And I am so grateful for the good fortune of having as parents the hardest working people in America! My education and determination was the outcome of their fine example and this book is also a salute to their compassionate spirit. To my father and mother I say . . . En memoria de mi padre Javier, que supo brindarnos su amistad y cariño, uniendo a nuestra familia y así ganándose el amor de todos. Y finalmente para la mujer valiente y brillante que ha inspirado mi pasado, presente y seguirá inspirando mi futuro, mi madre Zobeida . . . siempre serás una luz alumbrando mi camino.

As this book is about the importance of social support in promoting the well-being of individuals I must say that I have been most fortunate to have a number of unofficial mentors at the Calfornia State University at Bakersfield, that have guided my professional development. For their advice, direction and support I give warm thanks to my colleagues and friends Dr. Vandana Kohli, Dr. Gonzalo Santos and Dr. Thomas Martinez; each in their own way have contributed to my growth as an academician and have safeguarded my overall well-being. To use a colloquial phrase, "I got lucky when I met them!"

And special thanks to researchers at the RAND Corporation, Dr. Paul Koegel and Dr. Audrey Burnam, for the invaluable experience and training they provided for me while working as a consultant on their study, *The Course of Homelessness.*

Chapter One

Homeless, Not Hopeless: The Survival-Networks of Latino and African American Men

There is a tendency to view homeless individuals as marginal members of our society. However, even amidst their personal crisis many among the homeless maintain social relations that provide them with measurable access to needed resources, thus, enabling their daily survival (Johnson, et. al. 2005; Bao, et. al. 2000). In, *Homeless, Not Hopeless,* I explore the nature and scope of the social and/or personal networks utilized by homeless Latino and African American men, while also examining their ethnic group differences in the experience of homelessness. Fundamentally, social networks perform a supportive function and are often the vehicles through which resources are channeled to individuals. Social or personal networks among homeless men can be both formal (involving institutional or social service oriented sources of support) and informal in nature (involving kinship based and non-kin based sources of support)—this study focuses on the latter form. Also, these networks may range in scope from providing emotional to material support for their members. Therefore, the maintenance and reliance among homeless individuals on social networks is important to consider, if we are to better understand how they access and use various resources in negotiating their daily survival. The key premise of this book is that Latinos and African American men manage to survive homelessness by participating in social or personal networks which they access through the practice of an active agency that facilitates the activation of social capital embedded in these networks that then allows for the flow of resources; thus, homeless men negotiate the daily impact of extreme poverty on their lives.

In the U.S. homelessness is experienced by a diverse segment of the nation's population that is thought to include a disproportionate number of minorities (Burt, et. al. 2001; Rossi 1989; Bingham, et. al. 1987); however, this finding is

1

rather misleading. Although, there has been extensive research on the nature of African American homelessness, research highlighting ethnic group variations among the inner-city homeless has been very scarce. Specifically, research focusing on the situation of homelessness among Latinos has been notably absent, particularly since they represent a large segment of the minority population in the U.S. Initially my interest was to examine the role social networks plays in the daily survival of homeless individuals. Later I became interested in understanding the diverse situations of homelessness experienced by Latino and African American men. To this end, the primary questions guiding this work are as follows: "How do informal social networks operate for homeless Latino as compared to homeless African American men?" and "How are social networks initiated, maintained or weakened? In addition, a deeper exploration of the homeless experiences of Latinos requires that a further within-group distinction be made, that is, whether these individuals are recent immigrants to the United States, or long-term residents (and/or native born). Subsequently, in order to better capture the situation of homelessness that exists among Latino groups, a third question helped guide the present work, "How do the social networks of recent Latino immigrants (primarily mono-lingual Spanish speakers) compare to those of long-term residents and/or native-born Latinos (more Americanized, English speakers)?"

Furthermore, the network analytic approach taken here examines the personal networks of these men from the perspective of the individual participants interviewed (i.e., egocentric view of network traits and functions; see Frey, et. al. 1995). Given the time and funding constraints of this study, corroboration of these individual observations or self-reports by alters (the network members) was not attempted as this technique went beyond the scope of the present study. Still, the network analytic approach employed here provides a useful framework for understanding how people with extremely limited resources manage to survive homelessness on a daily basis. Specifically, examining how homeless men initiate, participate in, and maintain personal networks can increase our understanding of the purposive action taken by these men in negotiating their situations of homelessness and also of the role that even tenuous ties with both housed and homeless people may play in promoting their well being (Toohey, et. al. 2004; MacKnee and Mervyn 2002; Conley 1999).

UNDERSTANDING AND DEFINING HOMELESSNESS

In the last two decades of the twentieth century, homelessness was identified as a major social problem and subsequently, attempts were made to gain information on the social characteristics and the size of the population. During that time, the United States Census Bureau obtained estimates of the homeless population throughout the country, from which they derived a national homeless population estimate of 178,820 persons in emergency shelters and 49,793 persons at pre-identified street locations (U.S. Department of Commerce News 1991) (estimates barred enumerators from going onto rooftops, cars, dumpsters or any dangerous locations where homeless people might be found).

Regional and national estimates of the size of the "homeless" population vary based on the enumeration methodologies used to identify and count individuals. Commonly, individuals are identified as homeless if they lack regular night-time accommodations, and must rely on the use of shelters, transitional living programs, single resident occupancy hotels, public or outdoor facilities (parks, streets, under freeway overpasses, etc.), and/or sleep in cars, all-night theaters or abandoned buildings (McKinney-Vento Homeless Assistance Act 1987 and 2002; Rossi 1989). However, the U.S. Department of Housing and Urban Development (HUD) uses an expanded definition that includes persons who are on the verge of homelessness within a week's time. HUD considers the precarious situation of individuals who have very limited resources and expect to be evicted from their residence, discharged from an institution (e.g., hospital) or forced to leave their home due to domestic problems (e.g., violence) (HUD, ESG Desk guide, Section 4.4). Still others, like the U.S. Department of Education also consider the experiences of children and youths to be within the scope of homelessness, specifically those who: must move in with other family members or friends for reasons involving economic hardships or the loss of housing; must move into inadequate accommodations like motels/hotels, trailer parks or camping grounds; or must live in shelters (emergency or transitional); or those that are abandoned or waiting to be placed in foster care (Section 11434a of the McKinney-Vento Act).

Therefore, the methodological designs used by researchers and agencies in defining, locating and counting homeless individuals impact the estimates obtained of this population. In light of such diverging methodologies, in Los Angeles county an estimated 80,000 men, women and children are homeless each night (Burns, et. al. 2003; Los Angeles Homeless Services Authority 2003; State of California 2002), several reports indicate that L.A. has the greatest concentration of homelessness nationwide (Burns, et. al. 2003; Cousineau 2001) and that homelessness in L.A. is growing (requests for emergency shelter have increased by 15% among individuals and 21% among families) (U.S. Conference of Mayors 2004).

Nationwide efforts to understand the social world of homeless people reveal that homelessness is a gender-typed phenomenon (men are overrepresented,

80 to 90%), includes a disproportionate number of minorities (an estimated 40% are African Americans, 11 % are Latinos, 6% are Native American and 1% are of another ethnicity—compared to 40% who are White) and has a growing number of women and children within its ranks (Urban Institute 2001). Studies indicate that homeless men, generally: are single, without nuclear families; have either never married or they have experienced a break in a personal relationship; tend to have tenuous ties to extended family members; experience physical and mental disabilities that often go untreated (46% report a chronic physical condition and 22% report severe mental illness, 5 to 7% of which need to be institutionalized); are extremely impoverished with incomes that are 50% less than the official poverty line; suffer a series of long-term problems prior to the onset of homelessness, that include unemployment, a lack of affordable, and other interpersonal troubles noted above (Urban Institute 2001).

Social Networking and Activation of Social Capital

The national portrait emerging of the social world of homeless people while notably bleak is also more dynamic than these nationwide statistics indicate. The role of social support resources is crucial to the survival of homeless individuals. Whether social support resources are generated through interpersonal sources like family and non-kin networks or stem from access to a number of public assistance programs and/or social service providers, they are a vital part of surviving a life of homelessness. In any case, interpersonal network participation among homeless men can yield an array of emotional, financial and referral resources that can facilitate their survival (Molina 2000; Snow and Anderson 1993). For instance, the social networks of homeless people can help offset the stress and dangers associated with life on the streets (Johnson, et. al. 2005); however, networks that are primarily street-oriented can also increase the likelihood of risky behavior (Johnson, et. al. 2005; Snow and Anderson 1993). Still, the prevailing view in the literature underscores the supportive and beneficial aspects of network participation, particularly because networks can provide a safety net or temporary reprieve from extreme poverty (Toohey, et. al. 2004; MacKnee and Mervyn 2002). Strong and/or consistent social ties are particularly important for individuals with low levels of social and human capital (Waldinger 1999)—as is typically the situation of homeless men. Generally, effective network participation is linked to social capital activation. Social capital within networks is activated and transmitted by maintaining contact with and developing strong ties to network members (or relations) as their shared expectations of accumulated social debt and repayment generates a collective sense of group membership

(Lin 2001). Similarly, homeless men manage to activate social capital within their networks in this manner, albeit, they do experience greater networking obstacles.

This book presents a social psychological analysis of the personal networks and non-kin relationships maintained by homeless individuals whose daily lives are punctuated by the effects of extreme poverty. This analysis expands on the existing literature that counters stereotypic or individual deficit explanations of homelessness that tend to blame the victim (MacKnee and Mervyn 2002; Wright 2000; O'Flaherty 1996; Anderson and Snow 1993), by examining the purposive networking activity of homeless men. This study attempts to assess the means by which acutely impoverished individuals negotiate their situations of homelessness through the use of adaptive survival strategies centered on maintaining social ties that periodically alleviate the strains of life on the streets; although the networking of the extremely poor is not equipped to provide the economic support necessary to ensure a permanent exit out of homelessness. This approach is useful in understanding the social environments and behavioral routines of homeless people that can generate social support and resources (i.e., within the bounds of larger structural forces that produce extreme poverty). And while the analysis carried out here elucidates new conceptual and methodological directions for both homelessness and social network research precisely because it focuses on issues of active agency among homeless individuals (found in their daily negotiation of homelessness) that departs from an "overly-victimized view" on the extremely poor, the analysis should *not* be taken to imply that the networks of homeless men can carry the total burden of support—alone. Instead, the active agency of homeless men does imply that some (if not many) could benefit from greater provisions of institutional support that build on existing networking practices, thereby linking these men to communities of support in facilitating their transition into more conventional housing arrangements.

Furthermore, traditional homelessness research has portrayed homeless men as disaffiliated from society and from meaningful relationships that could provide them with a safety net during this crisis (Bahr 1973; Wallace 1965). Although, social disaffiliation does characterize the lives of some homeless individuals, too often deficit-driven analyses (or the "something lacking" views—like social disaffiliation notions that are discussed at length below) are imprecisely applied to all situations of homelessness. When employing a social network analytic approach this means that a "something lacking" view is used to assess the presence or absence of network properties or attributes (e.g., moderate or infrequent contact with family relations signifies family disaffiliation and an absence of family support); thus, minimizing or even ignoring the instrumental functions of network ties among impoverished people during times of crisis. This oversight creates methodological problems within network analysis because it obscures the role that network relationships play in the lives of extremely impoverished people by equating their network's "limited resource capacity" in absolute terms as indicating a "complete lack" of tangible resources. The complexities of homeless social worlds are made less intelligible when nuanced examination is substituted with an over-reliance on traditional assumptions. For instance, in line with traditional discourse or deficit-driven or something lacking perspectives that assumed homeless men were in fact completely disaffiliated from active and meaningful relationships, the present study followed a methodological course designed primarily to investigate the self-reported struggles of these men to survive homelessness (for more information refer to previous work, Molina 2000). And as the extent of networking practices among homeless men was unanticipated (given the prominence of the "disaffiliation" view in homelessness literature) the present study was not designed to triangulate (corroborate) their reports through interviews with alters (their network members). This conceptual and methodological oversight contributed to the following limitations of the present study: the attribute-based network analysis presented in this work relies empirically on self-reports without corroborations from network alters and thus, also provides only a snap shot view (cross sectional analysis) of their networking experiences.

Research Background and Interest in Homelessness

As a research consultant for the RAND Corporation (a nonprofit research organization in Santa Monica, California) during the mid-1990s, I acquired extensive field experience while working in Skid Row Los Angeles. Through my work with service providers and homeless individuals living in the area I gained invaluable access to the range of actors engaged in surviving or assisting in the situation of homelessness. Moreover, while working on the "Course of Homelessness Study" for the RAND Corporation, I spent over a year and a half interviewing, maintaining contact with and getting to know homeless individuals and these experiences facilitated the development and implementation of my own investigation of homelessness. Through this experience I became aware of ethnic group differences in the daily survival strategies of homeless minority-group members. That is, patterns of reliance on certain institutional services (whether bed or meal facilities), interpersonal contacts and the types of assistance obtained appeared to vary among Latinos and African Americans. After spending nearly two years observing the environment of Skid Row and examining much of the research on the experience of homelessness among minority groups (e.g., African Americans compared to Latinos—the two largest minority groups in the U.S.), I concluded that a closer examination of minority homelessness was needed in order to augment the scare and insufficient research generated about their situations. Thus, I decided to conduct an empirical investigation of ethnic differences in the experience of homelessness. Consequently, I spent another sixteen months among homeless people and service providers in both Skid Row and East Los Angeles conducting qualitative in-depth and semi-structured interviews and nonparticipant observations. A complete discussion of the methodology employed is found in the Appendix section of this book.

In order to identify individuals as homeless, I used the criteria of literal homelessness. That is, for the purposes of this study, individuals were considered literally homeless if they had spent even one night of the last 30 nights sleeping in: 1) a shelter or mission; 2) public outdoor places (streets, beaches and under freeway overpasses); and 3) in abandoned buildings or in cars and other vehicles (Rossi 1989). This is an operational definition for homelessness, philosophically being homeless entails much more than having no regular place to sleep. It involves adapting to a highly unconventional way of life. An adaptation to what many have called a subculture or even counterculture of street people (Snow and Anderson 1993; Wagner 1993). Subcultural ways that embody a repertoire of behavioral survival strategies, such as: engaging in shadow work (opportunistic sources for earning an income) (Snow and Anderson, 1993); the use of meal and bed facilities (Snow and Anderson 1993; Wagner 1993); the exchange of modest resources—including alcohol and illegal drugs (Snow and Anderson 1993); and the presence of tenuously held ties (Snow and Anderson 1993; Rossi 1989) and a few intimate ties as well (as I assert in the chapters that follow).

DEMOGRAPHIC TRAITS OF HOMELESS PARTICIPANTS

Table 1.1 presents demographic information on homeless Latino and African American men participating in this study. Beginning with the country of origin, we see that a third of Americanized Latinos were born in the U.S.A. and another third were born in Mexico. The Americanized sample of Latinos also consists of Central American (20%) and Puerto Rican men (20%). In comparison, recent-immigrant Latinos were overwhelming from Mexico, with only one Cuban individual among them. African American men were all born in the U.S.A. The average age of participants is 35.6 years for Americanized Latinos, 29.4 years for recent-immigrants and 44.9 for African Americans. Regarding education, neither Latino group completed the years equivalent to high school education in the U.S. (Americanized Latinos completed 8.9 years

Table 1.1.   Demographic Characteristics of Homeless Men by Ethnicity/Race

	Latino (Americanized)*	Latino (Recent-Immigrant)**	African American
Country of Origin (percent):			
U.S.A.:	30	-0-	100
Mexico:	30	91	-0-
Central American:	20	-0-	-0-
Puerto Rican:	20	-0-	-0-
Cuban:	-0-	09	-0-
Age (average yrs.):	35.9	29.4	44.9
Education Completed (average yrs.):	8.9	6.4	12.3
Age First Homeless (average yrs.):	31.2	19.7	36.6
Never Married (Percent):	60	55	55
Length of Current Homelessness (average yrs.):	2.0	2.0	3.0
Homeless Episodes (average no.):	4.0	7.0	3.0
Employment in Last 30 Days (percent):	50	73	26
Unemployment, Longest Episode (average yrs.):	1.7	1.3	7.0

*Refers to Americanized Latinos (primarily English speakers).
**Refers to Recent-immigrant Latinos (primarily Spanish speakers).

and recent-immigrant Latinos 6.4 years), compared to African Americans
who received 12.3 years of schooling.

Both Americanized Latinos and African American men first experienced
homelessness in their thirties (31.2 and 36.6 respectively, table 1.1). Recent-
immigrant Latinos, on average, became homeless at a much younger age
(19.7). More than half of the men in all three groups have never been married
(60% of Americanized Latinos and 55% of both recent-immigrant Latinos
and African Americans). At the time of the interviews, homeless Latino
groups had been currently homeless for approximately two years, and African
Americans were homeless a year longer than Latinos (an average of 3.0
years). Further, the all of these men had experienced several episodes of
homelessness—with recent-immigrant Latinos falling in and out of homelessness more frequently than their Americanized counterparts (4.0 episodes)
and African Americans (3.0 episodes) as well.

On average Latinos were able to obtain employment, within a specified 30 day period, more often than their African American counterparts (table 1.1 — 50% of Americanized Latinos worked for pay, compared to 26% of African Americans)—with the highest rate of employment reported by recent-immigrant Latinos (75% worked for pay). The longest episode of unemployment was reported by African Americans (an average of 7 years), followed by Americanized Latinos (an average of 1.7 years) and then recent-immigrant Latinos (an average of 1.3). The descriptive and narrative accounts presented in the chapters that follow illustrate the saliency of social and/or personal networking processes in the daily survival of homeless Latinos and African Americans whose experiences while dire are not without resolution.

What's Significant about the Social Networking Approach?

There has been a resurgence of interest in social network theories because such theories combine the social psychological interests in the individual with the broader structural interests in the situation. Social network analysis provides for the investigation of a fundamental sociological concept, social structure (Wellman 1983; McCarthy 2002). Network analysts focus on understanding the pattern of network ties among members that yield varying opportunities and constraints in the distribution of resources (Gottlieb 1981; Hirsh 1981; Wellman 1983). Thus within the network analytic perspective, "social systems are treated as networks of dependency relationships resulting from the differential possession of scarce resources at the nodes and the structured allocation of these resources at the ties" (Wellman 1983). Essentially network analysis goes beyond the study of dyadic ties to include more complex structural relations among actors. In an articulation of some of the basic principles of network analysis, Barry Wellman (1983:157) states:

> The most direct way to study a social structure is to analyze the patterns of ties linking its members. Network analysts search for deep structures — regular network patterns beneath the often complex surface of social systems. They try to describe these patterns and use their descriptions to learn how network structures constrain social behavior and social change. Their descriptions are based on the social network concept of ties linking nodes in a social system — ties that connect persons, groups, organizations, or clusters of ties. This emphasis on studying the structural properties of networks informs the ways in which analysts pose research questions, organize data collection and develop analytic methods.

Social network analysts regard the following assumptions as central to any examination of the form and content of social networks: 1) reciprocity among members differs in content and intensity, and for the most part network relationships tend to be asymmetrical (Cook 1981; Wellman 1992); 2) network resources are unevenly distributed given asymmetric ties and complex networks (Davis 1970); and 3) the network density or interconnectivity of network members varies by relational context (e.g., network density tends to be greatest among family members compared to friends or associates) (Wellman 1983; Oliver 1988).

Moreover, the network analysis carried out here examines the emergent structural properties of personal networks consisting of the following components: 1) the attributes of personal networks (e.g., size, functions, type and flow of resources); 2) the attributes of network relations (e.g., membership relationship types, social context of relationships, closeness, frequency of contact and reciprocity); and 3) the overall saliency of network participation (e.g., perceived benefits and liabilities of the instrumental aspects of network participation, and assessments of the overall saliency and purposive nature of their relationships involving levels of social intimacy) (Hurlbert, et. al. 2000; Emirbayer and Goodwin 1994; Oliver 1988; Wellman 1983). Studying the process of formation, maintenance and destruction of social networks among homeless men will offer greater clarification of the assumptions noted above as the next few chapters unfold. The capacity at which social networks operate, or cease to do so, for disadvantaged homeless groups is of particular interest because of the added strain their situation places on network members.

PERSPECTIVES ON HOMELESS PEOPLE

Indelible images of extreme poverty, isolation, and despair are intimately linked with the plight of homeless individuals and yet the question remains, "How do they manage to emotionally and physically survive their homeless crisis?" "How, indeed, do they survive life on the streets of Skid Row?" The informal social support networks that homeless men engage play an important role in facilitating their daily survival. However, this notion of social networks among the homeless seems ironic given historically common portrayals of these men as transients, as socially disaffiliated, isolated and as disempowered (Wallace 1965; Caplow 1940).

Two key theoretical approaches have emerged in the analyses of homelessness, disaffiliation and displacement models. An extensive discussion of each view is presented below, briefly stated for these theorists the problem of homelessness is couched either in terms of individual pathology and retreat from society (the view among disaffiliationists) or in terms of structural displacement and rejection from society (the view of displacement theorists).

Notably, in seeking to understand the situation of homelessness both theoretical camps are guilty of side-stepping or, at worst, of dismissing the issue of human agency. In this regard, taking a symbolic interactionist perspective can guard against generating strictly pathological or strictly structural interpretations of the nature of homelessness because of its focus on the meaningful and purposeful activities of individuals. For symbolic interactionists human agency is a central part of sociological inquiry, emphasizing the purposive and intentional nature of human action and survival.

Essentially, the concept of agency asserts the power of individuals to act both independently of structural determinants, as well as within such constraints (Giddens 1984). Furthermore, agency highlights the importance of human free will and raises issues of moral choice and political capacity (Gouldner 1973). In order to give human agency a central place within homelessness research, this book also considers the following questions, "How are homeless individuals making sense of their lives out on the streets?" and, "What actions, practical or otherwise are they taking to survive their bouts with homelessness?" These questions underscore the importance of analyzing what is meaningful, purposeful and practical in the daily lives of people experiencing homelessness. Essentially, the specific tenets proposed by symbolic interactionist for understanding human actors (presented below) contribute to a more empowering view of the much misunderstood and often much maligned people who find themselves homeless.

A Symbolic Interactionist Take on Homeless Actors

By stressing the importance of the active, interpretive, and constructive capacities (competence) of human actors—despite the impact that larger structural forces may have on their lives—symbolic interactionist bring the issue of *agency* back into the picture. For symbolic interactionist capturing what is meaningful to actors requires observation and analysis of the social processes from which such meanings are thought to emerge. Blumer (1969) summarizes the three basic premises first asserted by George Herbert Mead (the father of symbolic interaction), they are as follows: 1) "human beings act toward things on the basis of the meanings that things have for them"; 2) these meanings "arise out of social interaction"; and 3) social action results from a "fitting together of individual lines of action." Fundamentally, symbolic interactionist argue that human beings are intimately involved in constructing and reconstructing the social world through symbolic meaning, and therefore, that their individual efforts are essential to sociological inquiries. They remind us that it is people and not structures that create social order. In fact, this argument has contributed to the debate in sociology over the centrality of agency versus that of structure in explaining social action.

In the midst of such a debate, my own views are located in the recognition of the importance of both individual agency and structural determinacy. I see the relation between structure and agency as complementary, that is, as involving structural influences on human action and individual agency as capable of affecting social structural changes. I agree with Bhaskar's (1979) statement that, "Society is both the ever-present condition and the continually reproduced outcome of human agency."

EXPLAINING HOMELESSNESS: DISAFFILIATION VERSUS DISPLACEMENT THEORISTS

Early research generated by several disaffiliation theorists depicted homeless men as under socialized (Strauss 1946; Pittman and Gordon 1958) and retreatist (Merton 1949), in short, homeless men were viewed as social nomads. Yet others among them saw these men as acculturated into a Skid Row environment (Wallace 1965; Wiseman 1970) and a life style that relied heavily on shelters and soup kitchens for sustenance. Generally, disaffiliation theorists maintain that homeless individuals, to some extent, willfully disassociate from the larger society because they are socially or mentally incompetent, and/or have a variety of other interpersonal problems (i.e., drug abuse, physical and mental illness or other anti-social disorders). Moreover, an ensemble of interpersonal maladies among the homeless are seen as contributing to their difficulty in retaining social linkages. For instance, the work of Caplow (1940) and Bahr (1967) served as precursors to the widespread interpretations of homelessness as a form of deviance and social disaffiliation. Caplow (1940) imparts the position taken by many of his contemporaries at the time, regarding the Skid Row man, this way:

> Homelessness is a condition of detachment from society characterized by the absence or attenuation of the affiliative bonds that link settled persons to a network of interconnected social structures. . . . In general; homeless persons are poor, anomic, inert, and irresponsible. They command no resources, enjoy no esteem, and assume no burden of reciprocal obligations. Social action in the usual sense is impossible for them. (1940:10)

Such disaffiliationists, while drawing attention to the lack or scarcity of social ties among homeless persons, erroneously characterize their lives as deviant, unattached, isolated, and irresponsible. Subsequently, many of these researchers concentrate their efforts on revealing the anti-social and problematic personality traits existing among the homeless (Sosin 1992). According to Sosin (1992), as recently as the 1980s much of the work generated by researchers continued to turn toward these personality deficit explanations of homelessness. Generally, disaffiliationists view the interpersonal problems of homeless men as the causes and not the result of their long term poverty. Even when well intentioned, the work of these theorists has a tendency to blame the victims for their impoverished situation. By depicting the troubles and circumstances of homeless individuals as severely pathological, disaffiliationists in effect, strip them of their own human agency or at best agency is acknowledged in regrettable terms. All said these researchers view homeless individuals as existing in a state of perpetual physical and emotional disarray that leaves them without recourse amidst the hostility of a Skid Row world.

Inadvertently, by overemphasizing the sullen nature of their personal afflictions, early disaffiliation theorists may have helped forge the stereotypical view of homeless men as irresponsible derelicts. Given the portraits rendered by these theorists, homeless men lose twice over. Once, because of the severity of their homeless situation and twice based on the underlying assumption that due to their own excessive negligence, culpability rests with them alone. The remedy to homelessness or life on the streets, then, lies only in attempts at individual rehabilitation (the general position taken by old and new schools of disaffiliationists)—leaving the structural conditions that constrains individual options largely unaddressed (Wallace 1965; Crystal, et. al. 1982; Morse, et. al. 1985).

In response to disaffiliationists' views on homelessness, the contemporary school of displacement theorists (or dislocation theorists) emphasizes the impact of larger structural forces (i.e., economic dislocation and deindustrialization, government policies, or availability of affordable housing) in accounting for homelessness. These researchers simultaneously de-emphasize individual social pathologies as primarily causative (Ropers 1988; Rossi 1989; Belcher and DiBlasio 1990; Elliott and Krivo 1991). They argue that large-scale social, political and economic forces—which individuals have no control over—constrain the options and resources of impoverished people, leading some of them into homelessness. In a critical departure from the views of disaffiliationists, homeless individuals are not readily seen as blameworthy. However, they do tend to emerge as 'overly victimized' given the liabilities of such imposing structural forces (Wagner 1993; Rosenthal 1994). Once again the problem of agency emerges. A rigid structural analysis would, in effect, dismiss the question of agency among homeless individuals. Recently, displacement theorists have substantively and methodologically attempted to reconcile the issues of agency and structure, by exploring the everyday experiences, social relationships, and cultural understandings among homeless individuals manifested within the larger structural context (Hoch and Slayton 1989; Snow and Anderson 1993; Wagner 1993). Human agency is evident in the actions and intentions of homeless men as many initiate, participate in and maintain social support networks (Snow and Anderson 1993; Molina 2000). Hence, individual agency is not surrendered to structural determinacy.

RECONCILING ACTOR AND STRUCTURE

There is more to the daily survival of homelessness than is captured by strict disaffiliation or displacement theorists. Namely, there is the inescapable human process of negotiating one's social world. While researchers debate whether homeless men are loners or just semi-isolates, I was struck by their sociability. The difficulty of their situation and the brevity of our interaction did not hamper their willingness to share even intimate details about their lives. It turns out that their sociability makes for more than just interesting conversation, it is a highly functional adaptation tool. Interaction among homeless people in Skid Row is crucial for several reasons—it is a prerequisite to gaining information about services, meals and jobs; it is necessary in gaining material assistance from others; and such encounters sustain the intentionality and meaning of their social world. And the interpersonal social networks of homeless men designate the relational context within which such purposive interaction takes place. Social networks involving casual acquaintances, associates and friends are essential in the daily survival of people living on Skid Row.

Therefore, neither by will nor by circumstance is it accurate to say that homeless men live as social isolates, devoid of any meaningful relationships. That these men are living in a situation of extreme poverty does not by extension make them anti-social. That they have been displaced from many mainstream institutions, job markets and from their communities is, in the last analysis, the outcome of structural forces (large-scale social and economic trends like economic downsizing, outsourcing and economic restructuring as a new global economy solidifies), which in turn, set in motion troublesome paths of interpersonal problems with which homeless individuals actively struggle.

Having duly noted the problematic dismissal of individual agency in traditional and even contemporary studies of homelessness, this book addresses the problem by illustrating the ways in which homeless men indeed respond to society's structural constraints. That is, by observing the actions and noting the intentions of homeless men as they initiate, participate in and maintain social support networks—all as a means of survival. Furthermore, taking a social networking approach to the study of homelessness sheds light on the extent of social isolation or of outright retreatism experienced by homeless individuals. The social networks and networking practices of Latino and African American homeless men are analyzed with regard to several emergent structural properties commonly found within networks. These emergent structural properties are examined by reference to the following network components and their characteristics: 1) the attributes of non-kin social networks; 2) the attributes of network relations; and 3) the overall saliency of network participation (the study's methods and procedures are fully elaborated in the Appendix).[1]

The work presented in the chapters to follow primarily constitutes a qualitative research endeavor that examines the struggles of homeless Latinos and African Americans and the support they engage to survive. The qualitative data analyzed was generated through in-depth interviews; however, both survey and demographic data were also collected in order to provide a broader view of the lives of these homeless participants. In order to examine ethnic groups differences in the experiences of homelessness both African American men and Latino men were interviewed. Further, Latinos interviewed consisted of two groups of homeless men: 1) Americanized English speaking men who were either native-born or long-term residents of the United States; and 2) a group of recently immigrated men who were mono-lingual Spanish speakers that often indicated they were undocumented residents in the United States. The responses for each group (African Americans and the Latino groups) are presented comparatively throughout the body of this work.

My objectives in studying their experiences, social relationships and networking practices are as follows: 1) To provide a more comprehensive view of the role of social networks play in the daily survival of homeless minorities, by conducting a comparative study of Latinos and African Americans— as well as, a within group analysis of homeless recent immigrants and Americanized Latinos; 2) To understand the saliency of network participation among homeless minority groups, both in terms of the network's benefits and liabilities; 3) To examine the phenomena of minority-male homelessness in light of structural conditions operating in the new century (e.g., major increases in the size of minority populations in the U.S., continuing patterns of racial/ethnic inequality, economic restructuring and globalization); and 4) To employ this comprehensive analysis of minority-male homelessness to provide a framework for generating corrective policy measures that are better suited to the specific needs of diverse homeless populations.

NOTE

1. The network characteristics formulated here draw largely on the work of Barry Wellman (1983), "Network Analysis: Some Basic Principles," and that of Melvin Oliver (1988), "The Urban Black Community as Network: Toward a Social Network perspective."

Chapter Two

The Social World of Homeless African American and Latino Groups: Background Traits and Daily Struggles to Survive

The changing character of the homeless population is evident in the now larger numbers of minorities among the homeless. However, the generalized statement that minorities are overrepresented among the homeless obscures the existing ethnic variation. In many studies of the homeless African Americans emerge as an overrepresented group, in comparison to Latinos who tend to be underrepresented (Smith and Smith 2001; U.S. Conference of Mayors 2004; Gonzalez-Baker 1994; Ropers 1988). Studies on American homelessness that have provided information on the Latino segment of the homeless population, usually offer little more than a percent count of homeless Latinos in generating an ethnic group breakdown (Farr 1984; Wright, et. al. 1987; Rossi 1989). While, researchers have found that homelessness is the outcome of a long process involving unemployment and other hardships rather than the immediate precipitation of such problems (Burt, et. al. 2001; Rossi 1988), overall studies examining how homeless individuals fare on various dimensions of social isolation, use of public and private non-profit services, personal income and employment have generated very little data on ethnic variations. Consequently, most of the conclusions that many of these studies reached concerning minority homelessness are largely representative of the experiences of homeless African American individuals, rather than depicting the situation of other homeless minority groups.

Moreover, studies that have attempted to analyze ethnic group differences, give credence to the argument that African Americans and Latinos have diverse experiences of homelessness, which require further elaboration. Ethnic differences among homeless Latinos and African Americans were noted in terms of: 1) income from employment, with African Americans earning higher wages than Latinos (Rossi 1989); 2) the incident of mental illness is

lowest among Latinos than any other homeless group (Koegel, et. al. 1988);
3) the use of public assistance programs serving homeless people is lower
among Latinos compared to African Americans (Ropers 1988); and 4) alcoholism has a greater negative impact on African Americans than on Latinos
(alcoholism also has greater impact on homeless whites, with the highest rate
of alcohol related problems reported among American Indians)(Wright, et. al.
1987).

By avoiding a deeper analysis of ethnic variations among the homeless, the
salient issues and factors that distinguish the experiences of Latinos from
African American homeless groups are overlooked. For instance, studies that
include Latinos in their homeless estimates still do not address the importance
of accounting for differences within Latino populations in the U.S., such as,
their immigrant versus native-born backgrounds. To date there is a lack of accurate estimates of the size of homeless recent immigrants (possibly undocumented workers) compared to homeless native Latinos.

Moreover, many studies do not adequately specify whether Latinos in their
homeless sample are Central American, Cuban, Puerto Rican or Mexican.
These within group distinctions should be considered in analyzing the experiences of Latino groups, given their diverse social and economic incorporation within American society. The lack of accurate and more detailed data on
the nature of homelessness experienced by Latino groups obscures our
knowledge of American homelessness in general.

The minority group distinctions generated allow a greater understanding of
diverse homeless groups and thus, help direct research toward more focused
and informed endeavors (particularly in light of public policy matters affecting homeless individuals). Next, U.S. Census information is provided highlighting the diverse social and economic integration of African American and
Latino minority groups.

WHY ARE PEOPLE HOMELESS?

Over the last twenty years attempts to respond to the question, "Why are people homeless?" have either led to explanations focused on individuals or on
the social-structure. Notably, the approach taken becomes the basis of subse-
quent policy suggestions aimed at ameliorating homelessness. If the causes of
homelessness are attributed to individual deficiencies (e.g., emphasis on personal afflictions such as mental and/or physical disabilities; individual
deficits in character, motivation and substance abuse; and on low levels of
human capital), then remedies could involve either punitive measures that
blame the poor (casting them as undeserving as a means of discouraging

pathological behavior) or to attempts at "fixing" afflicted individuals (via rehabilitation programs offered by service providers).

Critics argue that individual-deficient models of homelessness tend to ignore the role of social-structural factors that include rising poverty rates, changes in the job market, inadequate human services, insufficient minimum wages, shortages in affordable housing and the gentrification of inner-cities (Wright 2000; Timmer, et. al. 1994; Yeich 1994). Greater progress might be made in understanding the causes of and selection into homelessness by exploring the influence of both micro and macro factors; that is, by noting the way individual behavior is shaped by larger structural forces that "create a population at risk for homelessness" where fortuitous circumstances and/or "defects of persons determine who within the at-risk population actually becomes homeless" (Wright, et. al. 1998). Wright and his colleagues (1998) underscore the point that outcomes are mistakenly taken as causes when individual deficit models are used to explain homelessness. This has serious policy implications. For example, a quick survey of U.S. policy responses to the growing homeless problem reveals many inadequacies and increasingly punitive approaches taken: 1) shelterization of homeless people (emergency responses focused primarily on shelter expansion efforts; McKinney Homeless Assistance Act in 1987); 2) increased criminalization of homeless through local ordinances prohibiting loitering, camping and panhandling (National Law Center on Homelessness and Poverty 1999; Barak 1992); and 3) containment policies that restrict the geographic movement of homeless individuals by enacting strict shelter regulations and concentrating needed services within the inner-city (Stark 1994).

Since corrective policy measures are generated based on the perceived causes of homelessness, a focus on individual pathologies alone would leave important social structural factors unaddressed and vice versa. Although, micro-level analyses of homelessness are designed to yield more comprehensive accounts of individual experiences (the focus of this paper), multileveled examinations (micro-macro analytical links) are required in order to recognize the complex pathways that lead to homelessness.

Figure 2.1, Diagram of the Macro and Micro Causes of Homelessness, provides a conceptual diagram of the most recognized pathways to homelessness and underscores the primacy of macro-level structural arrangements in generating socio-economic conditions that strongly impact on individual actions. On the far right of the diagram are the homeless individual outcomes of interest that range from adaptive and resourceful (e.g., engaging in social networking to maximize access to needed resources) (MacKnee and Mervyn 2002)—to deficient and disaffiliated (e.g., mental and physical disabilities; low skills; substance abuse and lacking social ties) (Bahr 1973; Wallace

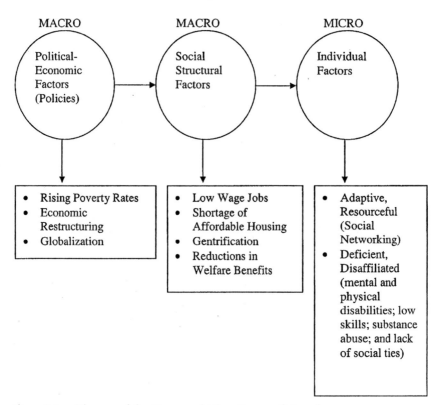

Figure 2.1. Diagram of the Macro and Micro Causes of Homelessness

1965). Influencing these individual factors are key social structural dimensions (e.g., low wage jobs, low stocks of affordable housing, gentrification of inner-cities, reductions in social welfare benefits) (Wright 2000; Barak 1992; Blau 1992). And as the far left of the diagram indicates, social structural factors are further determined by political-economic structures (e.g., dramatic income increases for the very wealthy and alarming drops in the real wages of the very poor, rising poverty rates, economic restructuring, and market policies involving globalization) (Wright 2000; Blau 1992). Briefly, the point stressed is that individual factors that contribute to homelessness must be understood as embedded within the larger social structural factors, which are further shaped by political-economic factors (economic and public measures adopted by elite policy makers) (Wright 2000; Barak 1992). Essentially, it is large scale structural arrangements that put already impoverished populations at risk for homelessness. It is important to fully understand the complex causal paths that generate homelessness and also that research conducted at any level helps to inform and expand other levels of analyses.

U.S. Population Characteristics for African Americans and Latinos

African Americans

The demographic, social and economic portrait of African Americans provided by McKinnon (2003) for the U.S. Census Bureau illuminates both the progress of the population, as well as, their significant socio-economic disadvantages they face compared to white Americans. According to McKinnon (2003) the African American resident population in the U.S. grew from 12.1 percent in 1990 to 13 percent in 2002 (or 36 million people). The U.S. Census 2000 shows an age structure difference among African Americans and white Americans, with a median age of 30.2 years and 37.7 years respectively. In regards to educational attainment among African Americans, 79 percent of individuals ages 25 and older earned at least a high school diploma compared to 89 percent of whites (McKinnon 2003). African Americans have made notable improvements in their college completion (i.e., bachelor's degree), 17 percent in 2002—up from 15.5 percent in 1990 and 8.0 percent in 1980. Among whites, 29 percent have completed at least a bachelor's degree (McKinnon 2003).

Since 1980, the labor force participation rate for African American males reveals two decades of stagnation, followed by a current downward trend: 70.6 percent in 1980, 70.1 percent in 1990 to 68 percent in 2002 (U.S. Census 1990 and 1989; McKinnon 2002 respectively). However, during this period the employment rate of white males also decreased from 78.2 percent in 1980, 76.9 percent in 1990 down to 73 percent in 2002 (still higher than that of African American men; U.S. Census 1990 and 1989; McKinnon 2003). In 2002, unemployment rate for African Americans was twice as high as their white counterparts (11 percent and 5 percent respectively).

There are also race and sex differences in the occupational distribution of African American compared to white American populations. Compared to white men, African American men are nearly twice as likely to be employed in the least appealing job positions as operators, fabricators and/or laborers (16 percent among white men and 28 percent among Black men; McKinnon 2003). While, most high-end managerial and professional specialty jobs are largely occupied by white men than black men (33 percent and 18 percent respectively). Similar proportions of male African Americans and whites occupy middle-range jobs involving technical, sales and administrative support positions in the labor market (20 percent).

Overall in terms of gender, white women fare better in the job market compared to Black women. Non-Hispanic white women are more likely to have managerial and professional specialty jobs than are African American women (37 percent compared to 26 percent, respectively; McKinnon 2003). These white women also have a greater command of middle-range jobs like technical, sales and administrative positions (40 percent among white women and 36 percent among black women). Conversely, African American women are more likely to occupy low-end service jobs (27 percent compared to 15 percent among white women), jobs as operators, fabricators and laborers (9 percent among black women compared with 5 percent among white women).

The occupational distribution of African Americans has a major impact on the population's overall economic well-being. According to a Current Population Report on consumer income in 2004 by DeNavas-Walt and her colleagues (2005), the median earnings of African American households constituted about 62 percent of the earnings of white households (approximately $30,000 and $49,000 respectively). African Americans have the highest rate of poverty in the nation (24.7 percent compared to non-Hispanic whites with 8.6 percent and Hispanics with 21.9 percent), indicating an adverse relationship between their income levels and the population's overall economic well-being (DeNavas-Walt, et. al. 2005).

From 1980 to 2003, the family composition of both African Americans and whites reveals a decline in married-couple family structure. According to the U.S. Census report on "America's Families and Living Arrangements" for 2003, married-couple families accounted for 47 percent of all African American family households and 81 percent of all white families (Fields 2004). When the 2003 CPR data is compared to 1990 and 1980 findings, it's clear that U.S. populations are experiencing a decline in married-couple households. For example, in 1990 married-couple families accounted for 50.2 percent of all African American families and 83.0 percent of all white families (U.S. Census 1990 and 1989). The 1990 married-couple family rate is down from the 1980 figures for both African American and white groups (55.5 percent for African Americans and 85.7 percent for whites; U.S. Census 1990 and 1989). Notably, the last decade has seen a decrease in the percent of female-headed, single-parent families for both African Americans and whites. The incident of one-parent, mother only, families decreased for African Americans from about 54.7 percent in 1990 to 45 percent in 2003 (U.S. Census 1990; Fields 2004). The corresponding figures for whites dropped from 19.2 percent in 1990 to 13 percent in 2003 (U.S. Census 1990; Fields 2004). There is reason to be optimistic about the drop in female single-parent families given that such family structures tend to experience higher poverty rates than two-parent families (a 2003 U.S. population rate of 28.4 percent compared to 5.5 percent, respectively; U.S. Census 2005).

Latinos

Not only are Latinos the fastest growing minority group in the U.S., they are also a very diverse group in terms of national origin. The U.S. Census data estimates the size of the Latino population in the U.S. as ranging from 37.4 million in 2002 (Ramirez and de la Cruz 2003) to 41.3 million in July of 2004 or 14 percent of the total population (U.S. Census Bureau 2005). The growth rate of the Hispanic population is so remarkable that Census reports state that, "One of every two people added to the nation's population between July 1, 2003 and July 1, 2004, were Hispanic" (U.S. Census Bureau 2005). Hispanics also represent the youngest of all ethnic populations in the U.S., with a median age of 25.8 compared to 30 for African Americans and 37 for whites (U.S. Census Bureau 2000). Furthermore, the Hispanic origin population in the U.S. is comprised diverse nationalities, with: 66.9 percent of Mexican origin, 14.3 percent are Central or South American, 8.6 percent are Puerto Rican, 3.7 percent are Cuban and 6.5 percent are of some "other Hispanic" origin (Ramirez and de la Cruz 2003).

Latino adults (25 years and older) have made some gains in their educational attainment since 1990. Specifically, Latinos increased their high school completion rates from under a 50 percent graduation rate in the 1990s to a 57 percent graduation rate in 2002 (U.S. Census 1990; Ramirez and de la Cruz 2003). Compared to a decade ago, Hispanics who earned a bachelor's degree increased from 9 percent to 11 percent (Ramirez and de la Cruz 2003); still their educational attainment remains lower than African Americans or non-Hispanic whites (17 percent and 29 percent respectively).

Since the 1980s, the unemployment rate among Latinos has declined by more than 50 percent (presently 8.1 percent rate of unemployment, compared to the rate of 16.5 percent in March 1983; Ramirez and de la Cruz 2003). Within group analysis of unemployment rates among Latino groups reveal that Puerto Ricans experienced the highest unemployment rates (9.6 percent), followed by "other Latinos" (8.6 percent), then by Mexicans (8.4 percent), Central and South Americans (6.8 percent) and Cubans (6.1 percent)(Ramirez de la Cruz 2003). Similar to African American men, the occupational distribution in 2002 of employed Latinos (20.8 percent) indicates that they were more likely to be employed as operators, fabricators or laborers than non-Hispanic whites (16 percent). Latinos were also more likely than whites to work in service occupations (22.1 percent compared to 11.6 percent among whites). Only 14.2 percent of Hispanics were employed in higher level jobs in management or the professions (those that tend to offer better pay, benefits and more prestige), while 35 percent of non-Hispanic whites occupied these positions (Ramirez and de la Cruz 2003).

In 2004, Hispanics earned a median income of $34,241 compared to the white median income of $48,977 in the same year (DeNavas-Walt, et. al. 2004). Poverty outcomes for Latinos, as affected by occupation and income levels, are more than twice as high as those of their white counterparts (21.9

percent compared with 8.6 percent), which includes an overall increase of 1.1 million in national poverty since 2003 (DeNavas-Walt, et. al. 2004). Further, the U.S. census reports that 68 percent of Hispanic households consisted of married-couple families, compared to 81 percent of their non-Hispanic white counterparts, while another 22 percent of Hispanics families consisted of single-parent, female-headed households (compared to 13 percent of similar white families; Fields 2003). Notably, U.S. Census reports tend not to distinguish between Latino cultural groups when generating demographic information about "Hispanics" and definitely do not disaggregate data in terms of "recent immigrants" (possibly illegally in the country), long-term legal residents and native-born Latino subpopulations.

CALIFORNIA'S IMMIGRANT LATINO POPULATION

The discussion to follow will focus on the experiences of the immigrant Mexican population in the southwestern U.S. because they represent the largest segment of the Latino population in the U.S. (67 percent of Latinos are of Mexican origin; Ramirez and de la Cruz 2003). Slightly over 12 million Hispanics call California home, Los Angeles County has the largest concentration of Hispanics in 2004 (4.6 million), and Mexican immigrants to California account for 10 million of the foreign-born people in the state (U.S. Census Bureau 2004; U.S. Census Bureau 2005).

In addition to the legally residing Mexican origin population in California, there exists an undocumented worker population that increases the overall size of this Latino population. In estimating the magnitude of the total population of undocumented workers in the U.S., Bean (Bean, et. al. 2002) uses a mid-range estimate of 7.8 million, of which he calculates 4.5 million are of Mexican origin (58 percent), with the other 3.8 million coming to the U.S. from other nations (including 20 percent from Central America). During the past decade the U.S. has experienced a rapid economic growth, thus its economy demands a large supply of low-wage workers and undocumented workers fill this economic niche—particularly in the Southwest (Bean, et. al. 2002). Given the needs of American capitalism, Presidents Bush and Fox (former President of Mexico) are engaged in serious consideration of new policy initiatives amenable to securing workers from Mexico through means that both serve U.S. interests and protect the rights of Mexican workers (Lowell and Suro 2002). Proposed policy initiatives would help regulate the flow of immigrant workers from Mexico by legalizing undocumented persons already residing in the U.S. and establishing legal measures to secure future labor migration.

According to a University of California, Los Angeles study (Marcelli, et. al. 1999), undocumented immigrant workers once thought to be an integral part only of informal labor markets, are now seen as integral to maintaining Los Angeles County's leading role as one of the world's most advanced economies. Undocumented workers, numbering in the hundreds of thousands, now occupy employment positions in a variety of occupational categories that include administrative assistants, health care technicians, retail salesperson, computer operator, typist—as well as, domestics, machine operators, farm workers, construction laborers and food service. Most importantly, through their presence in the informal labor market, these workers help to stimulate the formal economy (Marcelli, et. al. 1999).

An earlier study by RAND researchers supports the assertions of UCLA researchers, McCarthy and Valdez (1986) found that statewide Mexican immigrants fill the least skilled jobs (e.g., in agriculture and unskilled labor). However, in Los Angeles they also found that these workers increasingly occupy a large portion of semi-skilled positions in the manufacturing industries (in addition to farm work and labor jobs) and fill a share of craft and unskilled service jobs. Moreover, studies examining the effects of Mexican immigration on the public sector found that for both legal and illegal immigrant groups, their tax contributions actually exceed their use of services (McCarthy and Valdez 1986).

There are two points of interest in the study by Marcelli and his colleagues (1999), and McCarthy and Valdez' (1986) assessment of the impact of Mexican immigration on California's economy: first, overall state employment has been stimulated by their presence, because they are a source of low wage labor that encourages industrial and manufacturing growth; and secondly, they do not have a significant negative effect on native workers—other than their minimal impact on native Latino workers (i.e., lower wages). These demographic profiles illustrate the variations in the social, economic and educational disposition of legal residents as compared to undocumented immigrant Latino/Mexican populations in the U.S., which should be considered in analyzing the nature of their struggles with homelessness in the U.S.

Migration and the Role of Social Networks

The relevance of migration-systems theories to homelessness among Latinos (some of whom are likely to be recent immigrants), is linked to the manner in which such migrant networks transmit and shape the social, economic and political incorporation of these individuals in American society. An investigation of the socio-historical interrelations between sending and receiving nations provides the structural context within which immigrants formulate social support networks that impact their settlement and integration options.

The social, political and economic structural features of both sending and receiving societies are said to provide the originating impetus for migration. However, noteworthy explanations of the continuation, direction and persistence of migratory flows focus on individual and group participation in social networks that connect people across space (Portes, et. al. 1985). Classic 'push/pull' theories see migratory patterns (direction and size of flows) as a result of the social, economic and political backwardness of the sending nations, 'the push' (Portes and Borocz 1989). They further attribute 'the pull' of immigrants to host countries as the result of the labor demand and higher wages of these advanced nations (Portes and Borocz 1989).

Contrary to many of the assumptions of 'push/pull' theorists, Portes and his colleagues (1985) claim that it is historically established contacts between sending and receiving societies that provide a better account of migration flows. They assert that a strictly economic rationale for mass immigration cannot explain why large flows continue even after the economic incentives for such have significantly decreased (Portes, et. al. 1985). Essentially, international labor migration keenly involves a social process, wherein migrants generate social migration networks through their movement and contact with friends and family across geographic regions (Portes, et. al. 1985; Massey, et. al. 1987). Further evidence is provided by Massey and his colleagues (1987) that social networks not only help generate and sustain migratory flows (they found that prior migrant experience is the major predictor of future migration within family units), they do so by providing would be migrants with information about the process itself. Initially these networks are small in size, limited to a few friends and family members in the host country, as the migratory experience grows so does the network and thus a critical mass of migrants and their extensive networks are established (Massey, et. al. 1987).

Increasing our understanding the role of immigrant and native Latinos in the U.S. labor market, will further enhance our understanding of the particular situation of homelessness faced by Latinos as compared to their African American counterparts in America. Homeless Latinos are a subset of the larger Latino population, which is economically characterized by an overwhelming concentration in secondary sector labor markets, low wages and little occupational mobility. Their labor market incorporation can and often does contribute to the impoverishment of Latinos in the U.S.—which places them at risk for becoming homeless.

Studying the Social World of Homeless People:
Social Linkages and Resource Exchanges

Recent studies examining the daily survival patterns of homeless men, found that few homeless men actually live as complete social isolates. Instead, one historical study of old men living on the Bowery, claims that at worst homeless men are relatively isolated when compared to housed individuals in the same region (Cohen and Sokolovsky 1989). Also, Bowery men commonly participated in social groupings (usually revolving around drinking) and 68 percent said they could count on their linkages for help. Like this early study, homelessness researcher on the complex social world of these men affirms that many of these men also sustain meaningful, intimate relationships (Toohey, et. al. 2004; MacKnee and Mervyn 2002; Bao, et. al. 2000).

Lovell (1984) also found that networks of social relationships exists among virtually all the homeless men she interviewed—thus, contributing to supportive, though meager, resources exchanges among them. Furthermore, Snow and Anderson's work (1993) revealed that street peers perform more than simply instrumental functions they are also expressively oriented relationships offering interpersonal self-validation. However, these researchers do note that, "Street relationships are plagued with instability" (Snow and Anderson 1993:174). More recent research suggests that many homeless individuals engage in efforts to maintain meaningful social relationships that provide access to resources that contribute to their wellbeing (Johnson, et. al. 2005; Toohey, et. al. 2004; Bao, et. al. 2000).

Homeless individuals who do lack viable social networks may owe this misfortune to the increased strain their situation places on family and non-kin relationships overtime (particularly if their linkages have limited economic means)(Rossi 1989). Or alternately, a diminished or complete lack of interpersonal sources of support could be due to their problems of substance abuse, mental illness and other anti-social behavior (Snow and Anderson 1993; Rossi 1989). Homelessness researchers have not attempted to adequately examine either scenario involving social network processes (particularly as it involves ethnic differences). Among homeless individuals the role of personal or social networks has been found to be, a valuable though inconsistent source of support (Johnson, et. al. 2005; Bao, et. al. 2000; Snow and Anderson 1993; Rossi 1989). And while growing research indicates the presence of social linkages and networking practices among homeless individuals, they still tend to lack a comparative ethnic group analysis. Nevertheless, they do clearly indicate that homeless people live in a relatively active social world.

The role of social support resources is crucial to the survival of extremely disadvantaged homeless individuals. Whether social support resources come from interpersonal sources, like family and/or non-kin networks or stem from access to a number of public assistance programs and social service providers (private, non-profit and social welfare agencies) they are a survival tool. In either case, these sources of support can potentially provide an array of emotional, financial and referral assistance to homeless individuals. The problem arising for homeless individuals has to do with the availability of various social support resources and the usefulness of these resources for specific homeless ethnic groups.

PROFILES OF THREE HOMELESS MEN:
THE PRACTICE AND PROCESS OF HOMELESS NETWORKING

The functioning of non-kin social networks among homeless participants in this study vary in the following respects: 1) the level of social intimacy and the interpersonal expectations of network members; 2) the type and distribution of resources; and 3) given differences in expectations among members, variance exists in the content and intensity of reciprocity. The presence of long-term, socially intimate relationships, or friends, as well as, that of more casual but instrumental relationships (e.g., casual acquaintances and associates) in the social networks of homeless men sets in motion supportive exchanges that are endowed with personally meaningful interactions. Many of their interactions, then, provide homeless participants with emotional support consisting of interpersonal and multiple-role validation, understanding, concern and companionship. And, within the veil of social intimacy, non-kin social networks yield a broad array of material resources for their members.

The following is a depiction of the practice and process of social networking among three homeless men, Art (African American), Martin (Americanized Latino) and Lucas (recent immigrant Latino), all of whom have network experiences that characteristically capture those exhibited by many participants in this study. To better illustrate their networking practices the information presented covers two time periods: first, their current homeless situation; and secondly, the last time they had a room or home of their own.

African American Social Networking: Art—age 48

Art, an African American man, braves the homeless episodes in his life with a little help from his non-kin network consisting of several close friends and many familiar acquaintances known by sight, not by name. At forty-eight years of age, Art has been periodically homeless about five times and has currently been street bound for seven months. His friends consist of two individuals whom he sees around Skid Row daily, Buddy and Sandy (Art's girl-friend). The third person is his ex-wife Loretta who he is frequently in contact with, although she resides on the west-side of Los Angeles County—in the Santa Monica home they purchased when married. Art feels very close to his homeless friends, Buddy and Sandy (as well as to Loretta), because they have embraced him during both housed and homeless times.

Buddy and Art work together as truck loaders. Individually or jointly, they constantly survey warehouses and company loading docks for jobs and then pass on the day's employment news to each other. During the four years that Art has known Buddy he has repeatedly turned to his friend for some type of assistance that it's difficult for him to pinpoint just how often he's requested Buddy's support because, "it's an everyday thing." Although, they rarely ask one another for material support Art says, "That's my road . . . Buddy!" Given their difficult financial situation, these men seldom exchange monetary assistance (other than small amounts of money) and yet they do what they can for each other. Art appreciates Buddy's friendship and help:

> Just emotional help, you know nothing financial or anything like that . . . just emotional help. We share things like food and stuff like that. It's just like a daily thing. I don't ask for anything, we just . . . it comes up, if it happens it happens. Every day! [ed.] . . . I feel good that it's somebody I can share with, without any hassle. I can share things with somebody without either of us thinking that this has to be something . . . that you're doing this to get something in return. A lot of people do things just to get something in return.

Whenever Art needs to find Buddy he asks acquaintances around the Skid Row area if they have seen him and eventually, someone will get the message to Buddy that Art is looking for him. Together with Buddy and Sandy, Art and his friends have made downtown Los Angeles their hang out. These friends usually reside within four blocks of one another. Art describes their proximity as, "From here to across the street."

Sandy is one of two women in Art's network, who he says has been his friend and lover four years now. According to Art, he and Sandy share all resources acquired with each other, these include food, money, emotional support and sexual relations. Sandy, Art and Buddy often socialize together by going to the beach, movies and by just hanging out and getting intoxicated together. They often see each other at meal lines, shelters and generally around Skid Row. Loretta, however, is not personally acquainted with Buddy and Sandy, although she is aware of Art's relationship with them. Art regards his ex-wife Loretta as his closest friend and describes her as "a hell of a lady." And while, he hesitates to ask Loretta for any help, she usually surmises (when talking on the phone with him) what his needs are and encourages him to come "home." He has no plans to reconcile with his ex-wife, although he remains close to her and their children:

> See we own a home out in Santa Monica, her and my children stay there. I don't want to . . . I don't like to go ask her for anything. But I know if I ask her, she'd give it to me. She always let me know how my children are doing. If I need money or something from them, she'll give it to me. If I need clothes, something . . . she'll say come pick it up. She'll say just come on out here. Food, whatever I need.

Art says, "It's a fair exchange," meaning that he also tries to provide his friends with whatever support they might need. Art's survival on the streets of Skid Row is enhanced by the people he counts on for help who, while economically strapped, are willing to offer him any assistance they can. Art says, "There isn't any "wouldn't . . . they "couldn't" probably because they don't have it, but there's no "wouldn't."

Even back when Art was staying in a hotel room (about seven months ago), he was confident he could count on the support of his friends—Buddy, Sandy and Loretta. Art's relationship with these friends remains constant, and he feels as close to them now as he did during his last exit from homelessness when he managed to secure single-resident hotel room for a week's time. While residing at the single-resident hotel room, Sandy came to stay with him. During that time he visited Loretta in Santa Monica from time to time. Buddy and he would look for jobs around downtown Los Angeles. The only difference in his daily routine back then was that he turned did not turn to his friends for help as often because he was more financially stable. Art is quick to state that even when he had a place of his own, he tried to help his friends out on a daily basis.

Latino Social Networking: Martin, Americanized Latino—age 53

In the last six months Martin, a fifty-three year old native of Puerto Rico, has experienced several episodes of homelessness. In fact, he has been homeless off and on since the age of forty. Although, his network consists of both friends and associates, these individuals are not able to provide him with shelter and spare him the tour of missions and meal lines. Martin has spent many a night at local shelters; he's stayed at places like Bell Shelter (Salvation Army) and the Fred Jordan Mission where he currently resides as part of a Christian men's program.

After his allotted time in residence expired at Bell Shelter, Martin went back to his "old stomping grounds" where he slept under the stars at a city park. Martin slept outdoors for about a month and recalls not having so much as a blanket to shelter him from the cold. He recants his transition from shelter to streets and back to the shelter again:

> When I first went in [to Bell Shelter] it was different, it was like just what the name implies . . . a shelter out of the rain, out of the bad weather. Little by little it kept improving . . . a barber shop, library, a weight lifting room . . . cubicles for students! They had courses in school that you could take while you were there. They want you to be saving money so you could better your life. I went to school . . . I graduated from school . . . a retail sales manager. But then I have what they call "an addictive personality" and I was horse gambler. And I never saved any money while I was there, and I didn't plan for the future. After that, my time came to leave. I didn't have nothing going for me. I didn't have no money saved up so I started drinking again. I went back to my old stomping grounds. There was this church that I was going to sporadically when I was at the shelter and the pastor knew me. So, he found me sleeping in the park. I don't remember even having a blanket or a cardboard or anything. I don't know it was like God put me in a suspended animation for almost thirty days. Then he [the pastor] gave me a ride over here [to Fred Jordan Mission]. And I've been here ever since.

During this difficult time, when other options for shelter were closed to him and the local park became his nightly home, it was his friends Linda and Mike that reaffirmed their support for him by providing emotional and financial support. Martin never asked them for money, he visited them at their work sites and in seeing his condition they readily offered financial assistance. His relationships with Mike and Linda predate his experience of homelessness; these are the people that knew him when . . . when the future seemed bright, when time was on his side, when nights did not appear so endless. Now these friends are witnesses to this difficult episode in his life and as friends they do what they can to lessen their friend's burden, provided he lets them to intervene. Feeling down about his situation, Martin purposely avoids his friends—he says it's been several months since he last saw either of them.

In contrast to his infrequent contact with friends, Martin does keep in more frequent contact with many of his "street associates." These associates are his contemporaries in homelessness—Joe, Roy and Garcia are a few of the associates in his network that he's known for over five years (this is a lifetime for men struggling with situations of homelessness). One other member of his network, Jessie, is a recent acquaintance that he's known for only four months. Martin met Jessie while staying at the Fred Jordan Mission. Martin's network is neither large in size nor densely knit—only two of the five members in Martin's network know each other. Martin met Joe Garcia while hanging out and sleeping at a local park, in fact he says that he says that there were times when he used to spend the entire day hanging out with Joe at the park (before he was able to secure a shelter at the Fred Jordan Mission). Garcia is the custodian at the park where Martin stays most nights. Both Joe and Garcia have shared conversation, food, money and information about services with Martin and vice versa. He is closer to Joe, his drinking and Marijuana buddy, than he is to Garcia whose job it is to keep park safe for all visitors. Joe lives only a couple of miles away from the park where he and Martin usually meet. Martin describes his conversations with Joe as "uplifting" because Joe has expressed that he "thinks highly" of him for not giving up. He keeps Joe's phone number in his wallet in case he wants to contact him. As for Martin's relationship with Garcia, it's based on well defined role prescriptions— that of transient and park custodian, respectively. Each of them has learned to peacefully co-exist at the park. Martin respects the park rules (as enforced by Garcia) and Garcia lets Martin know if anyone comes by the park looking for him. From time to time Garcia shares his lunch with Martin, as these two men also share an understanding of their respective positions and manage to maintain good relations by respecting the parameters of their relationship.

Martin met his associate Roy, a housed African American man, during the time when he too had a place of his own and was steadily employed. Martin last saw Roy about six months ago. In recounting their relationship, Martin says,

> I know him enough to go to his house and say lend me ten dollars, and he would. But, like the park where I was, there's not too many Black people go around there so he wouldn't. He wouldn't go to my neighborhood. I go to his neighborhood and knock on his door. I would go and have a couple of drinks. We haven't had drinks for some time. He knew me when I used to work for Pep Boys . . . a counterman in parts, salesman. He knew me then, it was different. Because he keeps telling me when . . . "Man, look how you are man." He always had the impression that I was the manager, "Here you were the manager at Pep Boys," you know.

During the last four months since he's been participating in the men's program at Fred Jordan Mission, Martin has not been in contact with any of his associates or friends. The men's program at Fred Jordan Mission is a six month long, Christian rehabilitation program. While in the program, homeless men are not permitted any contact anyone except program members and staff workers. They provide meals, beds, work duties at the mission and intensive Bible study throughout the six month period.

Among the men participating in the program, Martin has become most acquainted with Jessie, whom he considers a close associate. Martin and Jessie talk about their problems, about getting back on the right track. Jessie is trying to turn his life around; he is an ex-drug addict who used to hang out on the streets. Martin respects what Jessie has to say because he recognizes that Jessie, like himself, has had a rough time on the streets of Skid Row:

We talk . . . we talk about Christian things. We talk about the world. He doesn't hold anything back, I don't hold anything back. Because I know that he's for real . . . The way he puts things, he gives you hope. You get to feel that it's hopeless, that these people never change but he did it. Last Sunday he gave a sermon, he spoke out in the church. He gave his testimony . . . the way he was changed from what he was to what he is now. Also, I identify with him. I was in a problem . . . I used to call my wife long distance and I used to go visit her. And then I will go back to the problem. Well he's doing the same thing. Like every Sunday he goes home and visits his wife and kids and then he comes back over here.

His relationship with Jessie has given him hope that he can improve his overall situation. He sees that Jessie is off of drugs now and that he has earned the respect of many members and staff in the program. Jessie has so changed his life that staff workers speak of sending him to Bible College to help him become a missionary for the Fred Jordan organization.

A year and a half has past since Martin last resided at his sister's home. He lived with her only a short while, about thirty days, and was asked to leave because he failed to financially contribute to the household. While staying at his sister's home, he continued to visit with his associates at the park and spend what little money he had on gambling. He says it's not that he gave up searching for a job, but rather that he simply could not find one. He referred to newspapers for employment listings (The Los Angeles Times); he had resumes and a letter of recommendation from his previous employer, but was still unsuccessful in finding a job. Employers usually said they would call him if they needed him, and they never called. It was soon after these unsuccessful job searches that Martin left his sister's house and went to stay at Bell Shelter.

Latino Social Networking: Lucas, Recent Immigrant—age 34

During both housed and homeless times, Lucas (a Mexican-born Latino) has maintained relationships with four men that he consistently turns to for help. His social network includes Martin, Luis, Beto and Shorty. Lucas and these men developed a friendship while watching soccer games at a local park. From that point on, Lucas says he enjoys spending his leisure time with these good friends just listening to Spanish music, watching sporting events or drinking socially together. According to Lucas he can count on the support of all four men[1] (quotes were translated from Spanish, see endnotes for Spanish language quotes):

I think that with the four . . . equally. Truthfully, if right now I went over there and asked for a taco or something . . . for them to allow me to stay a while . . . they would not deny me this. They would say yes. I feel embarrassed to go . . . many times I try not to go. But they, yes . . . all the time have said to me that when I need something . . . They have offered me to come into their house, in the living room. But I'm embarrassed . . . better I sleep in the car. It is their car. [Trans.]

Among these four friends, Lucas feels closest to Martin, his friend of two years. However, it was Beto, Luis and Shorty (who he has known since 1979) that introduced Martin to Lucas. Nevertheless, Lucas' friendship with Martin makes him feel as if they were childhood friends. Lucas says,[2]

I think that, like when we are small and one grew up with our friends. All the time we are together doing bad things, you know when we're kids. That's how I feel with Martin. [Trans.]

When Lucas wants to contact Martin he either walks to Martin's house or if he needs assistance (some type of help), he will arrange to meet him at the local park. Also, Lucas has the telephone numbers of all four friends and he usually phones those that live further away from the mission where he stays most often. Luis, Beto and Martin live within a four mile radius of Lucas' location, which makes walking to their homes feasible. His friend Shorty lives near South-Central Los Angeles which is only a short, bus ride away although Lucas avoids buses whenever possible:[3]

I have almost never liked going in the bus . . . Sometimes when I'm going far, yes. But like this nearby, I am always walking even if I have enough for the bus. [Trans.]

Lucas does not like to bother his friends too much because they have families to support, however, they have all done their share for him by providing him with meals, a place to spend the night, companionship, clothes, money on occasion and even information about jobs. Lucas recalls one incident in which his friend, Shorty, helped him find a job,[4]

He works for a company and one time he took me over there. Because he knows that I know a little about construction. And he spoke there to the manager. And he [the manager] told me yes and I worked only one day. Well, he paid me sixty dollars that day. He liked how I worked but he told me that my problem was that I needed some I.D. [identification card] . . . a social security card. Because, sense it's a company, they can't have people like that without social security or none of that. [Trans.]

His friends continuously inform him about job openings because they know he spends his days waiting on street corners for day labor or walking around town soliciting employment. Lately, it has been difficult for Lucas to find steady employment, he attributes this to the Immigration and Naturalization Department's amnesty program (department renamed to U.S. Citizenship and Immigration Services) which has financial sanctions against employers who knowingly hire immigrant workers that are either undocumented or are not registered for amnesty. Lucas says that the large companies only hire workers that have proper work permits or identification and employers that do not require these documents make promises of long-term employment, only to dismiss him after a few days:[5]

> Right now, like I told you the job is hard to get . . . they're paying too little in construction, for eight hours of work they pay me the day at fifty dollars. It's also difficult for me I don't have any I.D., or social security and then now with all that about the 'Amnesty'. A lot of the time they don't want to give us any [work] if we don't have 'Amnesty'. . . . Its difficult because when we get employed, many times they [employers] lie to us. [Saying that . . .] That they'll have work for about six months or maybe even a year. So they will see that we work well, one works fast. And when you least expect it, "No, you know what just three days . . . .two days . . . or a week and everything is finished." [Trans.]

Currently, Lucas says that there is little he can do for his friends, yet he still tries to reciprocate their efforts by helping them with chores and car repairs at their homes. His relationship with friends is built on mutual trust, respect and concern. Lucas says there has never been a time when they refused to help him because they know how hard he works to find employment and that he tries to supports them as well.

Seven months prior to becoming homeless, Lucas was renting an apartment room from an elderly woman. He lived in this Los Angeles apartment for thirty days, but soon after losing his job he ended up homeless out on the streets. Lucas' relationship with his four friends then was essentially as it is now, except that he is now unemployed:[6]

> The same as we are now. Well on the weekend we would see each other and we would drink beer to have a good time. Working, like I said for almost ninety days and since they worked too, we would get off tired. So we would see each other on weekends, Friday or Saturdays . . . Sometimes like I told you, for a good time we would go to a soccer match or something. Well, we had money so one of us would pay for one thing or another . . . that is, we would all contribute. No one would put in too much or too little, all were equal. [Trans.]

Whether housed or homeless the friendships in Lucas' life have remained constant. During times when he was employed and housed, it was he who supported his friends when they were short on funds; particularly since his

friends have families for whom they are the sole providers (wives and children). Fortunately, the group of friends that Lucas counted on for social and
recreational purposes in better days have served as a resource for him during
his homeless situation.

The social networks of these three homeless men highlight the distinctive nature of homelessness experienced by African Americans and Latino groups.
Moreover, having larger social networks is advantageous for homeless, African
American men—affording them greater alternatives for acquiring needed resources. Some researchers might interpret their networking as evidence of their
acculturation into a homeless, Skid Row way of life. However, many of their
network relationships were established prior to their homelessness. In many instances, the social networks of these African American men are a response to the
institutional constraints placed on them by service providers in Skid Row and to
the overall impact of the extreme poverty they face.

The social and/or personal networks of Americanized Latinos are nearly as
large as those of African Americans. However, the network ties of these Latinos are not privy to the same level of social intimacy as African Americans
experience in their relationships; notably Americanized Latino networks are
composed largely of associates and very few friends. For the most part, homeless Latinos dwell and engage in networking activities taking place literally
on the geographic outskirts of Skid Row L.A., unlike many homeless African
Americans in this study who negotiate their own survival by tapping on networks within such boundaries.

In contrast, homelessness among recent-immigrant Latinos seems to be an
altogether different matter. These Latinos are relatively recent-immigrants,
with a few long-term residents among them and whose primary concern is to
find employment in the U.S. They ultimately seek steady, full-time work but
settle for day labor jobs. They see their homelessness as a temporary situation
which they expect will be remedied through steady employment. Most of
these men had homes, that is, until they lost their jobs. And for a variety of
reasons, these men could not rely upon the migration chains typically available to recent immigrants (consisting of domiciled friends and family members) that provide housing support during periods of unemployment. For
these men securing employment in the U.S. is the key motivation for their migration to large urban centers (such as, downtown Los Angeles), where thriv-
ing businesses require large supplies of manual workers. These men, day laborers (most of which are undocumented workers), spend their days
searching for job opportunities, tending to avoid the meal and shelter facilities of Skid Row that could provide them with needed resources. These recent-immigrant Latinos are only peripherally connected to a Skid Row brand
of homelessness.

Based on these portraits of homeless men, we can conclude that while African Americans and Americanized Latinos (native-born and long-term residents; primarily English speakers) are largely displaced from mainstream social and economic institutions (family, job and housing markets) due to existing socio-economic structural constraints—homeless, recent-immigrant (Spanish speaking) Latinos are affected by issues related to: 1) international migration; 2) a lack of access to migration chains (or limited access); and 3) the socio-political climate in they encounter in the host country.

All groups negotiate the constraints of homelessness and thus larger structural constraints via their initiation, participation and maintenance of non-kin social networks. Elaborating on the dimensions of social networks, some theorists point to the intervening impact of social structural elements on the individual's networking:

> People create networks through a series of choices, and social structure influences their choices by determining the range and relative value of available alternatives. (Jackson 1977)

The structural determinants of poverty, such as unemployment, inadequate educational and job training, and the lack of affordable housing, while severely limiting the survival options of homeless men, has thankfully failed to seize their sense of personal agency.

If these men were completely cut off from society's mainstream resource pool (domiciled people, employment markets and service agencies), then we could correctly conclude that social structural forces had radically disempowered them. However, this is not the case. They actively engage both homeless and housed members of their non-kin networks on a frequent, if not daily basis. And although some may fit the bill, it is difficult to think of these homeless men as "retreatist." Furthermore, by retaining connections to housed friends, to service agencies and to employers they are in effect drawing on mainstream resources in order to survive. These homeless African American and Latino men act purposively to preserve their life-line to supportive friends, associates and casual acquaintances.

The visibility of those who are homeless within urban centers across America—as seen sleeping on city streets, lining up to receive a meal or in news media reports highlighting their troubles during winter months—has both heightened public attention and served to redirect research efforts toward the plight of extremely impoverished people. On the overall situation of homelessness in America, Wright (1989:89) states:

> Low incomes and high housing costs create a population at risk for homelessness, principally among those who are unaffiliated with households and other

social networks and among those who have been extremely poor for long periods of time. The homeless are the long-term very poor who have been unable to maintain supportive connections with (or have been rejected by) their parental families and friends and who have not been able for a variety of reasons to establish their own households.

I have set out in this study to examine the social network processes (both in terms of composition and content) of homeless Latinos and African Americans because I found that research on the situation of urban homelessness did not adequately articulate both the extent of isolation (lack of networks) and ethnic group differences (between and within groups) existing among people who experience homelessness. The substantive chapters that follow attempt to contribute toward correcting this oversight so that we might understand the full complexity of the situations of homelessness experienced and negotiated by America's two largest minority groups, Latinos and African Americans.

NOTES

1. Spanish quote: "Yo pienso que con los quarto por igual. Por lo sierto si ahorita voy para ya y le pido un taco o algo, que me den permiso de estarme un rato no me negan. Me dicen que si. Me da vergüenza ir asi, muchas de las veces trato de no ir. Pero ellos si todo el tiempo me han dicho que cuando necesite algo. Me han ofrecido que me meta alla a la casa, en la salla. Pero me da vergüenza . . . mejor me duermo en el carro. Es carro de ellos."

2. Spanish quote: "Pienso que como cuando esta uno chico asi que crecio uno con los amigos. Todo el tiempo andamos juntos haciendo maldades. Usted sabe cuando estamos chavalios. Asi me siento con Martin."

3. Spanish quote: "Casi nunca me a gustado andar en bús. A veces que cuando voy lejos, si. Pero asi serquitas asi, todo el tiempo ando caminado aunque tenga para el bús."

4. Spanish quote: "Shorty, como el trabaja en compañia una vez me llevo para ya. Porque sabe que yo se poco de construcion. Y hablo allí con el mayordomo. Y me dijo que si y trabaje no más un día. Que me pago sesenta dólares el día ese. Le gusto como trabaje pero me dijo que el problema mío era que necesitaba un I.D. . . . un seguro. Porque como es compañia y no pueden tener asi gente que no tenga seguro ni nada de eso."

5. Spanish quote: "Ahorita como le digo, el trabajo está muy duro. Están pagando muy . . . en la construcción, por ocho horas de trabajo me pagan el día a cincuenta dólares. Se me hace difícil también porque no tengo ningún I.D., ni seguro . . . y luego ahorita con eso de la 'Amnistía', muchas de las veces ya no quieren darle a uno si no tiene 'Amnistía'. Se me hace difícil porque cuando agarramos asi empleo, pues muchas de las veces nos echan mentiras . . . No, que van a tener trabajo por unos seis meses o tal vez un año. Según para que miren que uno trabaja bien, trabaja uno recio.

Y ya cuando menos piensa,"*No, sabe que no mas tres días* . . . *dos días* . . . *o una semana y se acaba.*"

   6. Spanish quote: "Igual de como estamos. Pues el fin de semana si nos mirábamos y tomamos una cerveza hay para darnos un buen rato. Trabajando como le digo casi como noventa días, nos mirábamos muchas de las veces entre semana nos mirábamos un día, dos días aquí en el parque. Como ellos trabajan también, pues sale uno cansado. Nos mirábamos más bien en fin de semana . . . un viernes o sábado. A veces como le digo queremos ir a divertirnos asi como mira un partido de fútbol o algo. Pues traemos dinero, uno pagaba una cosa otro otra cosa . . . o sea nos compartíamos. Nadien ponia de mas o de menos, todos parejos.

Chapter Three

Informal Non-Kin Networks among Homeless Men: Form and Functions

Whether housed or homeless, people are inherently social in nature. Inevitably, through our social encounters with acquaintances, associates, friends or family members we acquire a web of interpersonal social relationships. These relationships form the basis of our personal social networks. Social networks are a vital part of human survival, because they link individuals to society. Through their membership, networks can reach far beyond the individual's immediate scope, to generate a variety of supportive exchanges and resources. In this manner social networks become the vehicles through which individuals negotiate their social worlds. Even in dire circumstances, people often manage to connect with others in order to maximize their own survival and homeless men in this study represent a case in point. In fact, for many of these men life on the streets of Skid Row required frequent, if not daily, involvement in social networks. Networking can provide a safety net or temporary reprieve from the hardships of extreme poverty and there is mounting research that underscores the supportive and beneficial aspects of such practices among people that are homeless (Toohey, et. al. 2004; MacKnee and Mervyn 2002).

The analysis that follows derives from the overall perspective that social networks (consisting of intimate or even distant relationships) are a crucial part of the social fabric linking impoverished homeless men to opportunities and resources. Moreover, networks have been found to serve a number of positive functions: providing emotional and/or psychological support (MacKnee and Mervyn 2002; Bao, et. al. 2000); instrumental or subsistence support (Toohey, et. al. 2004); reduced depression (Bao, et. al. 2000; Unger, et. al. 1998); contact with mainstream society and conventional role modeling that enables exits from street life (MacKnee and Mervyn 2002; Rosenthal 1994; Grigsby, et. al. 1990); and accountability and increased self worth (MacKnee and Mervyn 2002). Given the socially supportive functions of social or personal networks noted above, it's clear that the absence of such social bonds can have serious implications for homeless people; researchers have noted that homeless people who replace lost family ties with street-oriented ties can become acculturated into a "homeless way of life" (Snow and Anderson 1992; Grisby, et. al. 1990). Notably, the presence of even one supportive and closely regarded family member or friend within the networks of homeless individuals resulted in greater success in exiting homelessness (MacKnee and Mervyn 2002; Mercier and Racine 1993).

From a social psychological perspective the nature and consequences of homelessness are best understood from the position of those affected (verstehen). Therefore, work presents a micro-level analysis of the personal networks and non-kin relationships maintained by homeless individuals whose daily lives are punctuated by the effects of extreme poverty. This analysis expands on the existing literature that counters stereotypic or individual deficit explanations of homelessness that tend to blame the victim (MacKnee and Mervyn 2002; Wright 2000; O'Flaherty 1996; Anderson and Snow 1993). Instead the present work attempts to assess the means by which acutely impoverished individuals negotiate and survive their situations of homelessness through the use of adaptive survival strategies centered on maintaining social ties. This approach is useful in understanding the social environments and behavioral routines of homeless people (set within the bounds of larger structural forces). However, it does not attempt to provide a causal analysis of homelessness. As I indicate in Chapter 1 the causes of homelessness (or extreme poverty) are within the purview of large scale social structural forces (the macro level imbalances in economic and political arrangements) that fail to generate living wages, sufficient stocks of affordable housing and social welfare safeguards for all people—including guaranteeing the right to housing. Also, while the findings presented here do grant insights into the social world of the homeless individuals interviewed, they cannot be automatically generalized to other homeless populations without taking into account various contextualized aspects. Still, this study's findings and conclusions could serve to develop a conceptual basis for generating more comprehensive research projects that examine causal relationships and also help develop corrective policy measures.

Also, while I argue that the social relationships of these men are neither completely opportunistic nor utilitarian in nature, the capacity for resource acquisition and mutual exchange generated by their networks is fundamental to their continual participation. I begin by redressing the oversight of much of the discourse on homelessness, that is, in omitting the integral aspect of human agency when describing the actions of homeless people. Here, I hope to clarify why it should not surprise us to learn that homeless men maintain the ability to protect their own interests in active and rational ways. Next, I review the social network approach and its analytical use of emergent structural properties. This section is followed by the major focus of the chapter—an analysis of the form and function of social networks among homeless Latino and African American men. I conclude with a discussion of the findings and the implications for each of the three ethnic/racial groups.

HOMELESS INDIVIDUALS AS RATIONAL ACTORS

Throughout this work you will find a resounding theme, one that I hope is neither overly deterministic nor strictly immersed in a kind of philosophical individualism.[1] It is the heuristic assumption that individual actors are rational decision makers who can and do negotiate their social worlds (with greater or lesser success). This theme echoes the ideas expressed earlier in the introduction regarding the complementary aspects of agency and structural determinacy, however, its specific relevance to social or personal network approaches bare repeating. Through the continuous, subjective, process of weighing the costs and benefits of particular social actions, homeless men (like most of us) act meaningfully to maximize their own self interests. These individuals make choices about whether it is preferable to initiate or to avoid a social encounter, to participate in and maintain a social relationship or to evade and dissolve the tie. Such practices demonstrate the workings of individual agency and its implied purposive, meaningful nature.

Further, it is within the limits of impeding structural forces that such choices are played out among homeless men (impact of structure on individuals); that is, within the bounds of extreme poverty, excessive unemployment, lack of affordable housing—within the constraining affects of homelessness—that behavioral choices are made.[2] Ultimately, such choices enable homeless men to establish a variety of relationships that link them to the wider society. Social or personal networks, then, emerge as a result of the choices individuals make within the limits of their environment. Most importantly, social networks reflect the ongoing negotiations of individuals struggling to reconstruct their worlds through a complex mesh of social relations.

NETWORK ANALYSIS: THE EMERGENT STRUCTURAL
PROPERTIES OF SOCIAL NETWORKS

A fundamental aspect of network studies is to analyze typically competing theoretical approaches, that is, to link the micro interests in individuals (social psychological perspectives) with the macro interests in broader social forces. Network analysts assert that social structures are best examined by studying the patterns of ties that link individuals to structures because it is within these structures that resources are obtained, restricted or denied (Hurlbert, et. al. 2000; Emirbayer and Goodwin 1994; Oliver 1988; Wellman 1983). Linkages between network members are usually asymmetric in the exchange of resources (varying in kind and amount) and overall relationships within networks tend to be asymmetrical as well (Cook 1981). Although network ties are characteristically asymmetrical (e.g., power differences, unbalanced capacity for resource exchange and levels of intimacy), some level of reciprocity in resource exchange among network members is nevertheless maintained, otherwise network ties dissolve (Wellman 1983). For a network analyst the scope of structural inquiry can range from the micro, social psychological (egocentric analysis), to the small group analysis of social networks, to the macro-level practices and patterns of social positions and connections within given societies. This book primarily examines the micro level experiences of individuals engaged in personal networking practices, and further contextualized their behavior by periodically interweaving a discussion of the macro structural arrangements that make such individual action necessary.

Form and Functions of Social Networks

In order to evaluate the extent to which social networking takes place among homeless men, participants in this study were first asked, "How many different people do you sometimes turn to for help?" Followed by extensive in-depth inquiries soliciting descriptions of their relationships, their emotional connection to the people in their lives, and the type of support or resources they acquired from their relationships. Furthermore, guided by the work of social network theorists (Fischer, et. al. 1977), the analysis presented below distinguishes both the emerging network properties or attributes (i.e., the attributes of the network as a whole that are not reducible to the individual link level) and the attributes of links (i.e., the characteristics of the relations which exist between individuals that are not reducible to a single individual). The social networks of three groups of homeless men (Americanized Latinos, recent-immigrant Latinos and African Americans) are analyzed with three fundamental areas in mind: the attributes of networks; the attributes of links; and the overall saliency of network ties. For analytical purposes each area is defined and composed of the following traits:

Attributes of Networks

1) Informal Networks: network membership involves informal ties with friends or casual affiliations (as opposed to formal networks which involve

linkages between service providers, organizations, or other agencies and their clients). These networks are often characterized by intimate and enduring social relationships. However, they also contain linkages between people who share little social intimacy and yet, provide each other with valuable resources.

2) Type and Flow of Network Resources: Resources or support generated by informal networks can be material (e.g., tangible resources like food, clothing, a place to stay, a place to wash-up and financial support) or expressive in nature (e.g., providing moral or emotional support, companionship, recreational socializing, or just someone to talk to).

3) Density: How tightly knit the network is, that is, the extent to which network members know one another. Density is the ratio of actual ties to all possible ties within a particular network.

Attributes of Links

1) Relationships: Types of relationships that exists within the network. The individuals or "nodes" participating in the network consists of casual acquaintances or associates (friendship linkages are discussed in Chapter 4). The links between these individuals establish the network's "ties." These "ties" can vary in social context (e.g., school acquaintance, church member or co-worker) and in strength (e.g., the level of social or emotional intensity associated with the tie).

2) Mode and Frequency of Contact: Type of contact used to communicate with members, for example, making contact with members in person (face to face), by phone, mail, through the intervention of another person, or any combination of these. And the frequency of contact maintained by members. The underlying assumption is that greater frequency of contact occurs among individuals with stronger interpersonal bonds or ties.

3) Closeness: The emotional intimacy existing within the relationship. How close members feel to their respective ties.

4) Reciprocity: The extent to which network members mutually support each other (emotionally or materially) or the extent of unidirectional support. Also, relationships can vary in reciprocity. That is, two people may differ in their value of one another to the extent that one person may regard the other as a "best friend," without a mutual correspondence from the other (different views on depth of relationship). The status of the friendship is thus, not reciprocal. This chapter examines reciprocity specifically with regard to resource exchange among network members and does not explore the extent of reciprocity present in such relationships, as doing so would require the collaboration of their friends or family members (alters) which went beyond the scope of this study.

Saliency of Network Participation

1) Network Benefits and Liabilities: Member's assessments of the utility of network participation. What they like and dislike about network members, functions or the networking process. Homeless network participants provide assessments of the network's resource exchanges (e.g., its capacity for exchange versus the actual acquisition of resources), members, rules, and normative prescriptions.
2) Saliency and purposive nature of the Relationship: Member's assessments of the meaning, purpose and level of social intimacy embedded within their interpersonal relationships.

The analysis that follows presents data on the network and link variables described above. It begins with a discussion of the manner in which homeless men distinguish between the types of relations found within their informal non-kin networks. After which, the findings are presented. The chapter concludes with a discussion of the implications of these results for homeless men.

INFORMAL NON-KIN NETWORKS

Homeless participants in this study have only a handful of people that they can count on for help and it is this handful that forms the basis of their social networks. The informal, non-kin networks of homeless participants in this study, consists of:

1) Relationships with friends that they have known for a long time and are highly regarded in terms of personal intimacy, loyalty and trust.
2) Relationships with associates that are characterized as much more superficial linkages compared to friends, and yet frequent contact and even a minimal emotional regard for these relations is maintained, usually through an active exchange of resources.
3) Relationships with casual or "satellite" acquaintances spanning the outer edges of Skid Row, relaying information to familiar yet detached others with whom they have minimal contact.

Homeless men very clearly distinguish between individuals that they consider friends and those who they regard as casual acquaintances. Yet, distinctions regarding their relationships with associates were more ambiguous. However, the term associate was heard echoing in many of the descriptions offered by the men interviewed and during observations of homeless men in Skid Row and East Los Angeles. The term associate was particularly prevalent among

English speaking homeless men (both African Americans and Latinos) interviewed at shelter facilities, perhaps resulting from the assimilation of the facilities' rhetoric. Although, recent-immigrant Latinos did not specifically use the
term associate in describing their relations with individuals who were perceived
as "closer acquaintances" but not "friends"—nevertheless, the term suitably de-
notes their characterizations of such relations. Using social intimacy as a measuring stick it is clear that associate-type relationships among homeless men
represent middle-range linkages, with friendships exhibiting high social intimacy and low intimacy among acquaintances. This hierarchy of relationships
(friends, associates and casual acquaintances) is analytically useful in concep-
tualizing the diverse relationships homeless men maintain. Descriptive statistics on informal social network variables are presented (see tables 3.1 and 3.2)
for African Americans, Americanized Latinos and recent-immigrant Latinos.

Surviving life on the streets of Los Angeles' Skid Row requires a good deal
of vigilance and sociability. Vigilance is needed to defend against the attacks
of poverty (i.e., threatened personal safety and sustenance) and sociability is
the means by which help is procured from unlikely others. Friends are
thought to be a rare commodity among the homeless, however through their
personal relationships homeless African Americans and Latinos have actually
gained emotional and material aid.

Findings

Table 3.1 presents data on the non-kin networks of homeless Americanized
Latinos, recent-immigrant Latinos and African Americans. As the table indicates, 90 percent of Americanized, homeless Latinos and 95 percent of homeless African American men have informal social networks. In contrast, recent-
immigrant Latinos exhibit a lower rate of network participation (82% have
networks). Turning our focus to Latino non-kin networks we find that their networks are relatively small, with an average network size of 5.6 for Americanized Latinos and 2.5 for recent-immigrant Latinos. The networks of homeless
Latinos are composed of more associates (100%) than friends (78%) among
Americanized Latinos and more friends (67%) than associates (44%) among
their recent-immigrant counterparts. Also, Americanized Latinos interact with
network members almost twice as often as do recent-immigrant Latinos (15.6
and 8.6 average days of contact per month, respectively). However, Americanized Latinos have known their friends for much less time (3.6 average years),
compared to their recent-immigrant counterparts (10.2 average years).

Furthermore, relationships with associates were better established among
Americanized Latinos (2.1 average years) compared to recent-immigrant
Latinos (0.31 average years—approximately 4 months).

Table 3.1. Characteristics of Informal Non-Kin Networks by Ethnicity/Race

	Latino (Americanized)* (N = 10)	Latino (Recent-Immigrant)** (N = 11)	African American (N = 20)
Percent with Non-Kin Networks:	90%	82%	95%
Average Net. Size	5.6	2.5	6.2
Type of Non-Kin Relationship: Percent with:			
Friends	78%	67%	84%
Associates	100%	44%	53%
Acquaintances	x	x	x
Frequency of Interaction: Average per Month			
Friends & Associates	15.6	8.6	16.7
Length of Relationship: Average No. of Years			
Friends	3.6	10.2	10.2
Associates	2.1	0.31	2.5

Notes:
*Refers to Americanized Latinos (primarily English speakers).
**Refers to Recent Immigrant Latinos (primarily Spanish speakers).
xRefers to an indiscriminate number of identified and unidentified, but familiar, casual acquaintances dwelling in regions of Los Angeles' Skid Row, down town and in East Los Angeles.

In comparison, a closer look at the non-kin networks of homeless African Americans reveals not only a high network participation, but also the largest network size (an average membership size of 6.2), and a network composed of more friends than associates (84% friendship linkages, compared to 53% with associate linkages). Their relationships with network members, like those of their Latino counterparts, are long standing. The longevity of their relationships is due in part to the high frequency of interaction they maintain with friends and associates (an average of 16.7 days per month), and to other supportive features characterizing their linkages. Moreover, on average they have known their friends for 10.2 years and their associates for 2.5 years.

Notably, for all groups of homeless men casual acquaintances were often referred to as people known on sight, rather than by name. Thus, casual acquaintances were as numerous for these men as are the span of meal-lines throughout Skid Row. Few among these men could identify their acquaintances by name (whether real or fictitious) and many were also unable to approximate the number of acquaintances with whom they regularly interacted; attesting to the broad range of such familiar faces among them. For these reasons, statistics estimating this component of their network membership could not be generated. Participants, however, commonly spoke of acquaintances as if they were permanent fixtures surrounding the landscape of missions and curb-side encampments found in Skid Row. Camouflaged with disheveled clothing and lackluster faces, the obvious residue of this harsh environment, many casual acquaintances are easily disregarded. They are granted little more attention than that pedestrians give to street signs—an occasional glance at rest stops and occasionally they are greeted with a grin, an upward tilt of the head and engaged in a quick exchange of the day's news.

The social networks of the poor, while less extensive and resourceful than those of higher income groups (Fischer 1982; Eckenrode 1983) can become elaborate resource exchange structures. Networking practices among low-income people are effective in their own right, often involving close relations (characteristically "strong ties" or family ties), a definite measure of mutual exchange or reciprocity among members, and at least a moderate degree of inter-connective ties or clear evidence of network density (Shapiro 1971; Fischer 1982). As noted in table 3.2, more than 75 percent of both Latino groups and nearly 75 percent of African Americans report having close relationships[3] with their network linkages. Also, most homeless participants report definite reciprocity,[4] or the unidirectional exchange of resources among network members (89% among Americanized Latinos, 78% for recent-immigrant Latinos and 79% for African Americans), which is a hallmark of strong social networks.

The number of inter-connective links that exist within the network, or network density,[5] is slightly higher among the Latinos groups (78% reports for

Table 3.2. Network and Relational Attributes by Ethnicity/Race

	Latino (Americanized)*	Latino (Recent-Immigrant)**	African American
Percent with:			
Close Relations:	78	89	74
Reciprocal Relations:	89	78	79
Network Density:	78	78	74
Type of Network Benefits:			
Emotional/Moral Support	45	45	84
Recreational	89	56	74
Illegal Drugs & Alcohol	67	11	37
Sustenance & Financial	67	78	79
Shelter/Temporary Housing	30	72	20
Protection	45	11	21
Job Info or Service Info	33	56	37

Notes:
*Refers to Americanized Latinos (primarily English speakers).
**Refers to Recent-Immigrant Latinos (primarily Spanish speakers).

both groups) than it is among African Americans (74%). Densely knit networks are important because they can increase the incidence of combined social support among members and promote greater adherence to group norms (Granovetter 1973; Craven and Wellman1973). Effective networking requires a minimum base of social relations that are equipped and willing to share resources (Auslander and Litwin 1988). Despite the relatively small size of their networks, homeless participants obtained material and emotionally supportive benefits from other homeless and housed network members. Table 3.2 also presents data on the traits of network relationships and on the benefits or resources generated through networking. First of all, the table indicates that 45 percent of both Latino groups and as high as 84 percent of African Americans participating in social networks received emotional and moral support. Second, an even higher percentage of these men spent recreational time in the company of network members (89% of Americanized Latinos; 56% of recent-immigrant Latinos; and 74% of African Americans). Third, social networks are also a means by which homeless men acquire and distribute illegal drugs and alcohol. This is particularly true for Americanized Latinos, who indicated they obtained mainly alcohol through their networks (67%); followed by African Americans who reported lower rates of alcohol use and slightly higher illegal drug use (37%); while, recent-immigrant Latinos reported the lowest rate of illegal drug and alcohol use (11%).

Networking also provides these men with resources vital to their survival (refer to Type of Network Benefits, table 3.2). At least two-thirds of all participants in this study report obtaining sustenance related (i.e., meals, clothing, cigarettes, soda . . . etc.) and financial support (i.e., monetary gifts or loans) from their network (67% of Americanized Latinos; 78% of recent-immigrant Latinos; and 79% of African Americans). Unfortunately, for two of the three groups of homeless men, networks were ill equipped to provide for the most immediate need—shelter. Whereas, 72 percent of recent-immigrant Latinos could turn to their networks for a temporary place to stay, Americanized Latinos and African Americans did not fare as well (only 30% and 20%, respectively, procured shelter from their networks). Also, personal safety or protection is a very real concern of homeless men living on the streets of Skid Row who, all to aware of the dangers, often opt to sleep outdoors only among familiar faces. Reliance on non-kin relations for personal protection is highest among Americanized Latinos (45%), followed by African Americans (21%), and recent-immigrant Latinos (11%). Furthermore, the social networks of homeless men are an important communication link providing them with information about jobs and/or other services available in their vicinity (a particularly important resource for 56% of recent-immigrant Latinos; and approximately one-third of both Americanized Latinos, 33%, and of African Americans, 37%).

With key features of effective social networking in place, homeless men actively raise the stakes on their own survival. Perhaps homeless men are often characterized as "disaffiliated" and "retreatist" because it seems inconceivable that people so severely afflicted by poverty—battling hunger, physical and psychological aliments, substance abuse problems and cold nights—can remain socially adept at maintaining personal relationships and at negotiating their survival. Yet this is precisely the daily personal struggle in which they engage.

Discussion: Non-Kin Networks

Although unenviable, the portrait emerging of these homeless men is hardly one of complete social isolation or of passive submission to a life of homelessness. The longevity of their relationships and high frequency with which they interact with friends, associates or acquaintances attests to their willingness and readiness to act socially on their own behalf. In comparison, aside from daily contact in the work place it seems safe to assume that few housed individuals contact their friends and associates with such frequency. Even if it were argued that the non-kin relationships of housed versus homeless individuals were substantively different enough to render such comparisons inconsequential—the surprising frequency of contact maintained by homeless people requires some explanation, which will be elaborated on in the next chapter. Suffice it to say that such explanations point to the presence of adaptive survival strategies.

The social networks of homeless men, in both form and function, illustrate that this is not a population so severely victimized by the structures of poverty that they have become inert and hopeless. Rather, in spite of being adversely affected by the limitations of poverty, they remain actively involved in their own survival and thus, are a population whose situation can be remedied through an effective national policy and social service intervention. The non-kin social networks of homeless men are endowed with benefits, liabilities and an erratic array of humble resources, yet membership provides them with substantial relief from their grievous circumstances. Even the non-kin networks of homeless recent-immigrant Latinos, which given their small membership size appear to be least well equipped to circulate resources to its members, nevertheless, provide these men with supportive resources that either exceed or are largely comparable to those received by their counterparts.

Overall, the social networks of homeless Latino groups and African Americans, while similar in a few respects, operate distinctively in generating specific types of resources for members. For instance, reports of reciprocity in resource exchange were high for all three groups. However, a closer look specifically at the resource exchanges of English speaking Latinos reveals a support system that is markedly different from those of Spanish speakers and closer in appearance to those of African Americans.

To review, the networks of Americanized Latinos consist primarily of associates who provide less emotional or moral support, but extend a good deal of recreational companionship coupled with a high incidence of illegal drug and alcohol exchanges (refer to table 3.2). Recall from the previous chapter, that most of these men suffer long-term episodes of homelessness (two years or more without a home). They also tend to spend their days procuring meals, clothing and shelter from the local missions and half of these men regularly take on odd jobs around Skid Row. Taken together, these experiences seem to indicate that Americanized Latinos have become increasingly acclimated to a Skid Row way of life. Some of these men have adapted to an aspect of street life and social relationships marked by what Snow and Anderson (1993:194) refers to as "Quick and easy conviviality and an ethos supporting the sharing of modest resources." Furthermore, while many can rely on their networks for sustenance and financial help, most of these Latinos cannot count on members for temporary housing or to relay information on jobs or other useful services; this is the expected result of a support network composed largely of homeless people (77% of their network members are also homeless). Here too we find evidence of their move, perhaps unwittingly, toward Skid Row behavioral orientations and away from those of the conventionally housed.

In contrast, while I resist the urge to crudely characterize some networks among homeless people as better than others, notably, the social networks of Spanish speaking Latinos are not readily identifiable as "typically homeless." That is, their networks are less oriented toward a Skid Row "life-style" (e.g., relying heavily on the services of meal and shelter facilities, panhandling, and frequent, recreational illegal drug use). Instead their networks are distinguished by close connections to housed individuals (most rely on "housed" network members for support, and many are provided with temporary housing by their friends), long-term relationships with friends and a strong orientation toward working for pay (73% report working within a 30 day period, compared to 50% of Americanized Latinos, and 26% of African Americans). They report low incidents of illegal drug use (and only 9% report having a problem with either illegal drugs or alcohol), and most spend the greater part of their day soliciting employment or working. Because they tend to identify themselves as workers (often taking on temporary or day labor jobs—for more information on undocumented immigrant workers in the U.S. see Leo Chavez 1992), their networks serve primarily as channels of communication geared toward job hunting (56% obtain job related information and/or information on other services through their networks—ranking highest among all three homeless groups).

The situation of homelessness experienced by recent-immigrant Latinos does not simply reflect ethnic distinctions it is fundamentally different from the prevailing depictions of American homelessness offered by researchers (Rossi 1989; Wright, et. al. 1989; Snow and Anderson 1993). While, some of these men are long-term U.S. residents, most are recent immigrants that migrated to the U.S. in search of work and for a variety of reasons are unable to draw upon traditionally supportive migration chains (Portes, et. al., 1985; Massey, et. al. 1987) that could shield them from homelessness. Nevertheless, their continuous association with housed network members and fellow day laborers seems to offer recent-immigrant Latinos a hopeful prospect for exiting homelessness.

Finally, a comprehensive view of the social networking endeavors of homeless African Americans reveals the presence of very definite "street survival" elements at work. Acquiring street smarts and allies is both a necessary function and condition of the nature of homelessness they experience. Networking is a particularly essential aspect of their survival because the majority of these men experience long-term bouts of homelessness, continuing for an average of three years or longer. And fully 100 percent of these men are involved in social networks containing a greater proportion of members that are homeless rather than housed (only 40% report associations with housed network members). Moreover, in the course of an ordinary day, most homeless African American men awake to the hustle of Skid Row shelters, meal facilities, panhandling and recreational activities with friends and acquaintances. Less than one-third of these men are able to secure employment throughout the course of a 30 day period, and self-reports of illegal drug use are highest among these men, although their overall rate of alcohol and illegal drug use is low. If these diverse group findings were aggregated into one "minority homelessness" pattern, then the results would be consistent with the typical portrait of minority homelessness in America that is often asserted by researchers (Snow and Anderson, 1993; Rossi 1989; Wright 1989; La Gory, et. al. 1989) and it would mask the varying experiences of homelessness revealed by comparative ethnic group analysis.

In sum, African American men suffer the effects of a particularly harsh and entrenched form of poverty and homelessness. Thus, it is these men for whom social networking is a necessary and essential element of daily survival. Perhaps this accounts for the high rate of social networking reported by African American men and also the high percentage among them obtaining emotional/moral support, recreational companionship, and sustenance and/or financial support through network participation. What is unobtainable from social service providers is procured through social networking channels, in either event, the costs and benefits of tapping resources is rationally assessed and is an integral part of their daily struggle to survive.

NOTES

1. Early sociologists (e.g., Tönnies, Durkheim among others) debated whether social order was best explained by reference to philosophical individualism, that is, by analytically prioritizing the role of individuals, or by examining larger societal forces. In their analysis, society won out. The actions of individuals were seen only as a secondary reaction to social forces—as constrained and defined by society itself. This represented a move away from the utilitarian and contractual tenets associated with philosophical individualism's notion of society and led to "simple mechanistic models of human behavior" or causal modeling (Fischer et al., 1977:04).

2. Within the context of particular social environments, individual rationality is further "bounded" (Fischer et al., 1977:42) in at least two ways: 1) individuals have limited knowledge of the universe of possible choices available to them; and 2) individuals sometimes incorrectly assess the particular benefit, or consequence, of available choices. And while some individuals may appear to act irrationally, they are still immersed in a continuous process of evaluating options and making choices deemed to be in their best interest.

3. The level of social intimacy, or closeness, among network members was derived from their categorical, yes or no, responses to the question, "Do you feel close to (name of affiliate)?" After which, they elaborated on the reasons for their responses.

4. Reciprocity among network members was measured through their categorical, yes or no, responses to the question, "Have you provided any kind of help for (name of affiliate)?" They were then asked to elaborate on their response, "Why?" or "Why not?"

5. Network density (or inter-connections) percentages for each group of homeless men were calculated by dividing the number of actual ties existing among network members (in addition to the participant), by the number of all possible ties. A 'tie' consists of at least two network members and the participant.

Chapter Four

The Saliency of Weak Ties:
The Acquaintances and Associates
of Homeless Men

Homeless men live in a complex social world. A world gripped by the forces of poverty, highly erratic employment, a shortage of affordable housing and the intrusive yet necessary presence of public service providers in their private lives. Yet their social world also engenders an array of meaningful social relations and resourceful exchanges. For this reason, the social relations of homeless men, and the web of interconnections they generate are intentionally given analytical primacy in examining their survival strategies. Because, it is through their relations (however tenuous, moderate or strong) that homeless people manage a life lived out on the streets. Even their weakest of ties (casual acquaintances) help define the nature of their existence in Skid Row. Through their relations they are variously identified as friends, foes, drinking buddies, panhandling partners, day laborers, or simply as familiar strangers. Their roles or positions subsequently confer upon them a myriad benefits and liabilities and thus, the very nature of their existence as homeless men is established.

Their relationships with street peers and/or housed affiliates are imbued with varying degrees of emotional intimacy and are often highly instrumental in their daily survival. More to the point, the social context of homelessness itself does not completely impede (although, it may limit) the development of a variety of social relationships among homeless people that enable their survival.

In fact, homeless men know who their friends are, and are not! They are quick to distinguish between various types of relationships. Personal levels of intimacy, trust and support mark the basis for such relational distinctions. Furthermore, there is a hierarchy of affiliations among street men, whereby, relations are ranked into at least three distinct categories: casual acquaintances, associates, or friends. This practice of differentiating among relationships is essentially an evaluative process in which homeless men assess the features or attributes of their interpersonal linkages and categorize them accordingly. Homeless participants in this study consistently distinguished among their relationships, providing a hierarchy of affiliations consisting of: casual acquaintances on the lower end of the attachment continuum; followed by middle-range linkages or associates; and culminating in the establishment of enduring relationships or friendships on the higher end (similar to the observations made by Cohen and Sokolovsky regarding homeless populations in 1989). And while this hierarchy includes all three types of social ties in this chapter the focus is on casual acquaintances and associates exclusively and reserve discussion of friendship-type linkages for the next chapter. The outcome of this process begins to reveal a social order in the seemingly random and chaotic world of homeless men—an order first nestled within their most intimate, which then radiates outward to the whole of their environment.

This chapter provides a qualitative examination of the non-kin network linkages of homeless Americanized and recent-immigrant Latinos and homeless African Americans. I begin with a discussion of network participation and then examine the saliency of weak ties. This substantive area is comprised of two major sections, the first on casual acquaintances and the second on associates. Within these sections, the analysis advanced is both multi-leveled and comprehensive in examining the following relational aspects: 1) social network relationships with regard to their attributes (e.g., the people known, the nature and development of bonds, the level of social intimacy, the extent of inter-connective ties, and the extent of reciprocity among ties); 2) the social context of network links (e.g., discussions of the social world or subculture of street life, the background of participants, the relational context—work peers, shelter-centered acquaintances, and/or recreational-companions); and 3) the ethnic/racial group variations and similarities within the overall analysis.

A final word on the analysis presented below. Essentially, it is a case study of homeless men examining aspects of their social lives, of their relationships, and of their interpersonal problems as well. This case study is not meant to be an indictment of the problematic lives of homeless men, wherein cases are presented as evidence of personal pathologies, rather, the intent is to illustrate the dynamic nature of their efforts at survival. To reveal how their daily survival is in fact a testament to their indispensable ingenuity in mediating the harsh structural poverty that surrounds them. And in this respect, the unexpected and intervening influence of various types of social linkages among homeless men is factored into analysis of their survival practices. The point here is that the poorest and most vulnerable among us ought to be seen from a better vantage point—one with a clear reverence for all aspects of their human struggle.

It was Max Weber (1922) who first espoused the methodological relevance of practicing verstehen; that is, developing an empathic understanding of the subjective experiences of actors by taking on the role of the "other" when observing and interpreting their behavior. Among homelessness researchers, it is Wagner (1993) who argues most ardently against employing an ethnocentric (and often middle-class) approach toward interpreting homelessness, because of its inherent tendency to focus on the pathology of "others" while dismissing the social structural dimensions of the problem. Wagner points out that social scientific research attempting to account for the interpersonal problems (i.e. mental health, substance abuse, or crime) of homeless individuals often, "tends to deny the potential social consciousness, political power, and humanity of the actual people involved" (Wagner, 1993:07).

Citing the work of Marcuse (1988), Wagner further cautions against falling into the ambiguous analytical practice of "specialism" (Marcuse, 1988:05), whereby the problem under investigation is cast as the sum total of a variety of "special" individual problems (e.g. problems of mental health, substance abuse or criminal behavior are seen as the cause and not the consequence of poverty and homelessness). In accord with the objective and sound methodological tenets of these researchers, I offer the following case study analysis of homeless men and their relationships as a means of understanding their social lives, their dynamic efforts to survive homelessness, and generally as a means of departing from an overly-victimized portrayal of people who are homeless. Instead, this analysis moves toward a more empowering view of these people who while arguably ill-equipped to exit homelessness still engage in daily attempts to survive their situations of extreme poverty.

NETWORK PARTICIPATION

Deciphering the nature of urban life (whether impoverished or otherwise) through an investigation of the complex ties that individuals construct, is precisely the domain of network analysis (Fischer, et. al. 1977). From this vantage point we become privy to the dynamic saliency of human relationships to social life and to the social structure. By reference to their participation in complex networks of relations, we are also better able to understand the purposeful behavior of actors. However, as Jackson indicates (1977), the range of "pools of possible intimates" available to individuals is limited by the social context in which they participate. Therefore, the relationships homeless men form are bound (to a greater or lesser degree) by their geographic location, their social position within the larger social structure, and by the very nature of their homelessness.

The Saliency of Weak Ties

Research focusing on the attributes of social relations has found that even weak ties offer important resources (Johnson, et. al. 2005; Toohey, et. al. 2004; Granovetter 1974; Katz 1966). For instance, Granovetter (1974) examined the nature of ties between job seekers and their contacts and found that people linked by weak ties gained greater employment opportunities than those linked by closer relations. This is accomplished through the interaction of weak ties (i.e., acquaintances and associates) with a variety of others, thereby establishing a broad web of relationships and of potential benefits among people that are linked directly or indirectly. In contrast, closer ties (i.e., intimate friends and family members) within an individual's social network tend to be connected to the same circle of people, resulting in more limited sources and circulation of information.

Individual social mobility in terms of jobs or other resources, then, is positively impacted by the strength of weak ties. Particularly among homeless men, the saliency of weak ties (e.g., casual acquaintances and associates) measurably rests on the capacity of such ties to expand their sources of information, which affects both the opportunities and actions of these men. And although these ties are tenuously held, they can potentially operate as a highly instrumental networking circuit radiating useful information from the outer margins of Skid Row to all interested parties. As illustrated in the sections that follow, the daily survival of homeless men hinges in part on the saliency and strength of their weak ties. In fact, such ties help define their existence in Skid Row, and so it is within the context of these ties (among their other linkages) that homeless men are made to belong in this social world. Because, embedded in the weak ties of homeless men we find the seeds of normative and behavioral prescriptions for living on Skid Row.

THE SOCIAL CONTEXT: SKID ROW AND NEIGHBORING LATINO ENCLAVES

Among homeless men, casual acquaintances are regarded with little intimacy, are the most tenuous of ties and are a numerous and inevitable part of the mix of shelters and soup kitchens in Skid Row. In fact, the Skid Row region of Los Angeles, which is just east of the city's central business district, has traditionally operated as a haven for homeless people. Skid Row is home to a large number of single resident occupancy hotels (approximately 4,200), shelters and soup kitchens, transitional shelters, small businesses and merchants (Shelter Partnership 1994). Further, on any given night the County of Los

Angeles is, perhaps unwittingly, host to an estimated 80,000 men, women and
children that are homeless (Los Angeles Homeless Services Authority 2003;
State of California 2002; Flaming and Haydamack 2003). And most of these
homeless people are concentrated in L.A.'s Skid Row area, partially thanks to
the city's "homeless containment policy" which funnels grant monies almost
exclusively into services for this region (Heskin 1987; Shelter Partnership
1994). It is within the context of this environment, that many homeless individuals become socially acquainted with those similarly situated others that
share a common fate.

Still other homeless individuals make only occasional visits into Skid Row
to obtain services (e.g., meals, clothing, showers), opting instead for services
provided on its outskirts. Such is the case for many Latino participants in this
study, who seek shelter in traditionally Hispanic areas of Los Angeles (e.g.,
La Placita on Olvera Street or Dolores Mission in East Los Angeles). Furthermore, homeless Latinos (particularly monolingual Spanish speakers—or
recent-immigrants) choosing to congregate in geographic regions that contain
a high population density of housed Latinos, increase their capacity to interact with local residents at parks, churches or at neighborhood stores. In this
way, Latino enclaves enable homeless Latinos to blend into the community
spatially and to some extent experientially as well. Within this social context,
homeless Latinos find a haven best suited to their cultural experiences. That
is, one that allows them to live out their days in synch with cultural values
and thus, enable them to appear less visibly homeless. Turning to Dolores
Mission, a Catholic church, for assistance or accepting sandwiches from a
meal van on Olvera Street while in the company of other Latinos is for these
men more acceptable than soliciting help from Skid Row providers. Relying
on the latter for subsistence would solidify their status as homeless men,
thereby, making them like "los indigentes" or the destitute living on the
row—people with whom they do not want to be identified. Their preference
for Latino geographic regions and aversion to being identified as homeless
means many homeless Latinos are more likely to develop relations and social
networks with other Latinos. Whether homeless men chose to dwell in Skid
Row or other neighboring areas, the social context in which they coexist
shapes their interactions and their relationships which in turn, impact their behavioral routines and overall survival adaptations.

CASUAL ACQUAINTANCES: THE SATELLITE LINK

Among homeless men in this study, casual acquaintances are serendipitously
acquired relations that are loosely formulated and carry few, if any, behav-

ioral expectations or interpersonal obligations, are numerously found throughout Skid Row and are seldom individually identified by name. The data presented below indicate that this type of linkage corresponds to traditional descriptions offered by researchers, portraying relations among homeless people typically as superficial and impermanent, or viewing their ties as strictly tenuous (Snow and Anderson 1993; Rossi 1989; Cohen and Sokolovsky 1989). However, not all relations among homeless men fit this pattern. Further, inasmuch as casual acquaintances have the capacity to transmit useful information throughout their social milieu they are highly effectual. Nonetheless these relations do retain a very remote social character, exchanging little emotional intimacy.

Acquaintances consist of people that inspire only a semblance of familiarity among homeless individuals, given their common exposure to shelters, service providers and life on the streets. The value of these ties lies in their satellite-like function, that is, in their capacity for receiving and transmitting information throughout the environments of homeless people. In regards to material resources, homeless men rely on acquaintances for little more than pocket change, a cigarette smoke, or a couple of drinks of malt liquor or fortified wine. Even the extent of reciprocity among homeless men and their acquaintances is confined to the exchange of information and/or some behavioral acknowledgement of each other's presence. Nevertheless, the resounding character of these interactions is that they lack a personal, intimate attachment.

Incidental Meetings

Oftentimes relations with acquaintances are as incidental as are the circumstances in which homeless people meet and yet they play an important role in circulating useful information. For instance, Michael is a thirty-four year old African American whose primary contact with homeless peers takes place within shelters and soup kitchens. Michael recently came to Los Angeles from Iowa, where he resided in his aunt's home. He has been periodically homeless since age thirty, staying in the homes of relatives and friends. For the last three months, Michael has been hanging out in L.A.'s Skid Row area and having few relationships, he describes the extent of his interaction with another homeless man named Bill:

> He's not a friend. It's just somebody that I pass by on the streets . . . I met him over a hot bowl of soup, to put it in a nutshell. I just met him over a feeding and it's not like I hang out with him. We're just acquaintances.

Michael runs into Bill at meal facilities where he spends no more than ten
to fifteen minutes in his company. The brevity of interaction among these
men in part results from the quick shuffling of homeless men through meal
facilities, and in part is due to their own desire to keep only minimal contact
with each other. Still, the organizational aspects of service providers (e.g.
meal and shelter facilities) often constrain the opportunities of homeless men
for forming and keeping social ties. However, with time even these brief
meetings and information-based exchanges among men can set the stage for
the development of closer ties and, as social network activity is concerned
they can also lead to an expanded scope of information and resource gathering. In Michael's case, he basically regards his interaction with Bill as "an exchange of information relationship." They grant each other little more than information about services available in the area.

Essentially, homeless acquaintances become each other's eyes and ears—
each constantly gathering information from one area and circulating to those
in another. Further, the information acquaintances circulate is seldom trivial.
In fact, it is vital to the survival of homeless men, because on any given night
it can mean the difference between spending the night out on cold streets, or
in a shelter known to have available beds. Cold weather shelters are constantly opening and closing, shelters fluctuate in the services they can offer,
new meal distributions points are springing up all over town—and with all
these changes occurring homeless individuals require a web of relations to
help them keep apprised of the events taking place.

Similarly, there is an incidental quality to the encounters of homeless
Latino men and their acquaintances. Although, among some Latinos such
linkages take shape within an ecological and ethnic context that is strikingly
different from that of L.A.'s Skid Row. Yet, the incidental nature of their relations with acquaintances remains. These men may become acquainted
simply by passing one another by on the streets and engaging in superficial
interactions. Linkages formed under such conditions are noticeably tentative,
situationally bound and fragile.

Aside from seeing familiar faces around areas commonly frequented
by homeless men (i.e., shelters, meal line and Skid Row streets), recent-
immigrant Latinos (primarily Spanish speakers that are either recent immigrants or long-term residents) and a handful of Americanized Latinos as well,
run into acquaintances at street corners where they go in search of day labor.
And much like that occurring in other homeless meeting places, interaction
among these men and their acquaintances on local 'day-labor' street corners
is brief and superficial. Dolores Mission, located just east of Skid Row, caters
to homeless Latinos. Here these men share a little conversation and occasionally information about jobs. For the most part, they like to keep to them-

selves. Other Latinos strike up conversations with acquaintances met at local neighborhood parks, churches and at recreational places (e.g., La Placita on Olvera Street). In general, through the course of their days homeless Latinos acquire acquaintances while alternating from the world of Skid Row to the familiarity of their ethnic enclave.

For Rafael (an Americanized Mexican American—currently homeless for seven months), casually encountering people out on the Skid Row streets gives him the opportunity to hear the latest issues or events making news among his homeless compeers:

> I'm an easy going person, if I find you on the street and you say "hi" to me, I say "hi" to you and that's it. If somebody is talking about politics or things like that I get close because I'm one of those persons that want to hear something to learn.

Yet another homeless man, Carlos (an Americanized, Mexican immigrant and long-term resident in the U.S.), makes the most of his incidental meetings with acquaintances who share similar interests by engaging them in what he refers to as "satisfying conversation." Although he enjoys socializing with casual acquaintances, Carlos makes no attempt to formalize relations and sometimes even neglects to ask a person's name:

> Yeah, there's another gentleman . . . I think he sleeps here on the streets. I don't think I even asked him his name. I like his conversation because he likes to speak about the Lord Jesus Christ . . . Godly conversation. Because anybody else that I [*speak to*] . . . wants to . . . sometimes I meet people here on the streets and they like to curse and swear and speak in ungodly style. I cannot support that kind of stuff.

Rafael and Carlos interact with acquaintances on a more recreational than utilitarian basis. In the world of the down and out, having people that one may share a little conversation with becomes a valued experience. Subsequently, like Rafael and Carlos, many seize the opportunity to become socially acquainted with some of their homeless peers, thus, making their presence known around town and in common hang outs. Establishing their presence within this social milieu broadens the extent of their interconnections with acquaintances (whether casual or otherwise). This simple social act in effect integrates them within the world of homeless men which, in turn, may prove to be much more instrumental to their survival than their initial meetings might indicate.

In varying degrees, both homeless Latinos and African Americans interact at least superficially with several street acquaintances and inevitably choose to do so within their own personal comfort zones. Because encounters among homeless acquaintances are truly casual, these types of linkages reflect the typically incidental nature of contact made on the streets. However, recurrent contact among even the most casual acquaintances fosters a familiarity that soon leads them to mutually identify each other as insiders, thereby, increasing their access to the homeless information network.

Familiar Strangers

Broadly defined, casual acquaintances or familiar strangers can include anyone who seems to belong in Skid Row, such as, local merchants or transients making their rounds through town. Both Latino and African American groups depict casual acquaintances as socially distant affiliations, lacking social intimacy and incidentally encountered around Skid Row. According to Ray, an African American man who has experienced a decade of homelessness, homeless individuals share information about the coming and going of recognized, but unknown people living in the area:

> You become conscious of the disappearance of people out here that you may not even know. But if you don't see a guy for a little while out here, then you start kind of quietly enquiring about him. You wanted to know whether he get busted? Is he alright? Something happen to him? Is he having trouble?

Like his homeless peers, Ray vigilantly charts the flow of people in his surroundings. Awareness of people, merchants and service agencies in the area helps expedite individual negotiations of available resources and functions as a personal protective mechanism. Knowing who belongs within his homeless milieu and who does not, also gives Ray leverage in sizing up potential problems and their resolutions.

Latino men that use shelters or meal facilities regularly, also express an awareness of familiar Skid Row dwellers. For Raul, a twenty-three year old recent immigrant who speaks English well, such awareness involves knowing the familiar strangers with whom he shares a sleeping site out on the streets. Getting to know others within sleeping encampments usually requires little more than a friendly nightly greeting; however, assurance that these individuals can be trusted develops over time. Raul knows very little about the three people that sleep in the same encampment where he does, and what he knows is enough to encourage him to keep his distance. And while many of their names are unknown to him, he is aware that they come from somewhere in Central America, "maybe from Honduras," and that they drink too much. Raul is acquainted with them by way of few hellos, but basically he keeps to himself because:

They work for drinking, drinking, drinking! I don't like that . . . everybody that's here is a liar. Everybody's too much problems. I looking for work to eat in different restaurants.

Informally monitoring the activity of familiar strangers serves as a protective mechanism and as a reference point. For instance, Latinos often refer to their acquaintances by their country of origin, which provides a common ground between themselves and the familiar strangers nearby. In lieu of a name they may identify an acquaintance as fellow countrymen, that is, as a Cubano (Cuban), a Salvadoreño (Salvadoran), or Mexicano (Mexican). This grants homeless Latinos a sense of ethnic and experiential commonality that almost transcends their homeless status.

What's in a Name?

We have seen that Latinos and African American homeless men engage in greetings or casual conversation with familiar strangers that are caught up in similar circumstances. Also, we have noted that their connection to acquaintances is characteristically incidental and tenuous. Yet another notable characteristic of these weak ties involves the tendency of mutual, casual acquaintances to disregard each other's names. Moreover, among the most tenuous of ties obtaining the name of acquaintances is purposely trivialized. Getting on with the business of survival makes it necessary for individuals to selectively befriend some and socially distance themselves from others in Skid Row. Not knowing the name of a casual acquaintance limits the level of familiarity between these individuals, thereby mutually freeing them from further unwanted social responsibilities. Deric's experience is illustrative. He is an African American man who although steadily employed, recently became homeless. On a particularly cold day on Skid Row, he told me that he hangs out alone most days and has a couple of acquaintances that he knows on sight only:

I have two people that, I don't even know their names. Only when I see them I say, "What's happening homeboy," real quick and that's it. Then we see each other on the streets again, I usually don't run with nobody. I usually stay by myself a lot.

Barely two months have passed since Deric left his room at the Frontier Hotel, a single resident occupancy hotel (SRO). The SRO where he lived is located in the heart of Skid Row, yet Deric made little effort to associate with people in the area. Because he works nights at the University of Southern California hospital (County U.S.C. hospital) as a custodian, after work he spends the rest of his day trying to get enough to eat and enough sleep at nearby parks before returning to work the following night. This routine leaves him with little time to strike up new acquaintances or friendships. In fact, he claims to have only one friend, some associates at work and at least two casual acquaintances.

While it is not surprising that men casually meeting up or sleeping out on the streets may fail to exchange names, you would expect that men who spend the day panhandling together would know each other's name. Max, an elderly native born Mexican American man, panhandles with people he meets out in Skid Row, yet he seldom knows their names. Knowing the names of fellow panhandlers seems trivial to him, because he has no intent of developing close linkages to these men:

> We panhandle together . . . after that you get drunk a little bit and disappear. You say, "Okay I go that way . . . Okay, thank you very much and nice meeting you." And that's it! I see different people every day. Sometimes I see the same guy, once or two times a day . . . I don't know these people. It's a homeless . . . people on the streets. Yeah, that's it . . . people like me.

The non-identification of individuals by name creates a greater social distance among affiliates. For men whose private lives are lived on public streets, this trend toward remaining *nameless*: restores a measure of personal privacy; frees them from many behavioral expectations or obligations; and maintains their anonymity with regard to the police and other authorities (Bittner 1967); and generally nullifies the intimate symbolic representation of their existence, so that the homeless actor is held as the object but not the subject of social inquiry. The unidentified, nameless man on the streets is neither completely propelled into the future, nor entirely embodied in the past because he is never fully part of the social discourse of others. In other words, these nameless men exist but are not completely socially present—without a name, their place in time is obscured. Returning to Max's panhandling experiences with nameless others, we see the ease with which these temporary companions bid each other well and then disengage from their relations—disappearing into some existence unknown, where perhaps they will meet again or perhaps not.

In other incidents, the names of acquaintances were known and they were sought out for recreational purposes, however, these individuals were still regarded as non-intimate strangers. After two years of being homeless, Tony (an African American male) has slept in his share of card board boxes and periodically resides in single resident occupancy hotels (SRO's). Basically, Tony became acquainted with a few individuals during lunch time at the missions and at Skid Row parks. Sometimes Tony goes to the local park to take part in card or domino games with acquaintances. Tony describes the nature of his street affiliations this way:

> No . . . there's no close relationships or anything that I had when I lived out on the streets. I was more or less a loner, you know I stayed to myself . . . I had acquaintances.

Currently, Tony is staying at the Dome Village homeless shelter (established by Justice-Ville U.S.A.) which is located on the outskirts of Skid Row. Prior to taking up residence at the Dome Village he spent his recreational time with his acquaintances Danny, Evelyn and Ernestine. Although he now resides at Dome Village, he still occasionally visits with these acquaintances. Tony's connections with acquaintances involves attempts at recurrent recreational contact, nevertheless, he makes it clear that they do not share socially intimate relationships. According to Tony, they are simply not his friends.

Among these homeless men, casual acquaintances represent the most tenuous of ties, yielding little in the way of emotional or material support. Because such casual acquaintances display low levels or a complete lack of personal intimacy, no significant attachments are formed among these types of affiliates. Typically, casual acquaintances involve people who inadvertently meet through exposure to street life, service providers, or are recognizably a part of the Skid Row milieu. Even when acquaintances are sought out, without the development of a greater degree of social intimacy these linkages remain at best superficial and at worst trivial. And yet, they function effectively, particularly as information messengers and are a crucial part of the survival mechanism of homeless men.

ASSOCIATES: THE UTILITARIAN LINK

Associate type linkages mark a social intimacy gray area. Although, associates-type linkages generate particularly instrumental exchange functions (i.e., providing material and financial resources), they are often afforded shallow to moderate emotional regard and are clearly set apart from those linkages considered friendships (which are imbued with high social intimacy and are discussed at length in the following chapter). Notably, through their web of relations these loosely knit linkages have the potential to tap a larger radius of resources and information, that is, compared to networks consisting of more closely knit linkages (i.e. friends and family members). Among homeless men, however, social networks comprised of associates are more limited in the range of potential contacts and sometimes in the types of resources they can provide (e.g., limited information and service related resources), than those containing a large pool of casual acquaintances. Generally, associate-type linkages tend to be utilitarian based relations that are intimate enough to insure the capacity for resource exchange, yet socially distant enough to give them a highly exploitative capacity as well.

Moreover, the associates of homeless men are people whose status lies between that of casual acquaintances and friends. Associates by their nature are more ambiguously defined than are affiliations at either extreme. Unlike the casual acquaintances of homeless individuals, which distinctly lack intimate, personal attachments and provide little if any material support—they characterize associates as people who: they have usually known for approximately six months or more; they have some degree of personal attachment to; and that provide them with varying levels of support and limited reciprocal exchanges. Compared to casual acquaintances, associates are closer and more well established social linkages.

Whereas, associates and friends share some defining features, the latter consists of more emotionally meaningful, enduring relationships. In many cases, associates cannot be counted on for help with the same regularity that friends can and they are not frequented as often as are friends. In all cases, they inspire lower levels of trust, respect, affection and concern than friends do; and overall their saliency tends to lie in their compensatory function rather than in their interpersonal connection.

Although relationships with associates offer less in the way of socially intimate interaction, because they can also function in a supportive capacity many homeless Latinos (mostly Americanized Latinos) and African American men come to rely on the support of such linkages—particularly in the absence of friends. In fact, the social networks of Americanized Latinos are largely represented by associate-type linkages, more so than recent-immigrant Latinos (who have very few associates) and African Americans (who have the largest social networks). Moreover, among Americanized Latinos associates represent key sources of sustenance and recreational support, unlike both recent-immigrant Latinos and African Americans who can also count on the support of friends. Interestingly, both Americanized Latinos and African Americans maintain associate-type relationships predominantly with other homeless individuals, while, the associates of recent-immigrant Latinos (like most of their friends) are housed individuals.

Gate Keepers of Life on the Streets

The social relationships of homeless individuals play a vital role in acclimating these men to the subculture of street life, that is, to the "patterned set of behaviors, routines and orientations that are adaptive responses to the predicament of homelessness itself and to the associated conditions of street life," (Snow and Anderson, 1993:76). It is particularly important for men who have recently become homeless to develop street-based affiliations with individuals who have substantial experience surviving out on the streets. Usually, individuals who have been homeless long term are well informed about available services and resources in their area, and also cognizant of the need to secure an effective survival strategy. Fortunately, given the extent of their experience, they are often willing to serve as gate keepers—helping recently homeless men adapt to street life. Moreover, associate-type linkages are well suited for this task because they tend to maintain frequent contact (especially, compared to acquaintances) and therefore, are available to provide more immediate assistance.

Tony, a thirty-six year old, African American man who has been homeless for two years, spoke of his relationships with two associates, Kevin and Art—one of which familiarized him with street life. He says about Kevin, "he's just a guy that I met at a parking lot, I talk to a lot." He does not consider him a close relation or anything of the sort, although he meets up with Kevin quite often around Skid Row. His relationship with Art is a different matter—as associates, they have a closer relationship. Grateful for all the help that Art has given him, Tony would like to refer to Art as a friend, but he still does not see him as such. For Tony friendship entails much more than is present in their relationship:

> Art would probably be different, the closest one out of all of them. He showed me the ropes, how to get in here [*refers to the shelter*]. When I first came downtown he told me all the places to eat, like the missions and stuff like that. He told me about Skid Row, because I guess he's been in Skid Row for like six years. I only been here two years. When I first came to Skid Row . . . he told me about the places to eat, the places to go get clothes, the places to be at the right time . . . [*edited*] He seen that I was living on the street and he's a guy that basically knew about all the places that you could go for help . . . he's a homeless person. Other than giving me information about Skid Row, about programs and services . . . No, no other kind of relationship. Ever since I've been living on the streets I never really call nobody a real close . . . somebody that I can depend on, in a life and death situation you know. He's just been a close associate.

Art has provided Tony with very useful information regarding Skid Row services, information that has been crucial in helping Tony acclimate to life on the Row. In return, Tony offers Art "a good card game" and this is the extent of their relationship. These men never exchange money or anything other than information and some recreational time.

ASYMMETRICAL POWER RELATIONS

All relationships involve exchanges of benefits and costs, however, when exchanges among individuals are unbalanced then asymmetrical power relations may develop. Such power differentials among affiliates, in turn, can lead to the exploitation of one by the other. As Jackson (1977) notes, "Equality of resources largely depends on equality of social positions." Therefore, homeless men engaged in asymmetrical relationships are particularly susceptible to exploitation. And it is the associates of homeless men that are most apt to exploit them, given common descriptions of these bonds as utilitarian-based, seldom emotionally intimate and yet regularly frequented.

For instance, a deep appreciation and a sense of indebtedness was not enough to inspire Daniel, a recently homeless Latino (Americanized), to look upon his associate Juan as a friend. Daniel arrived in Los Angeles three months ago—homeless and with little cash. Prior to this, he had a steady job in Minnesota for a period of three years he was able to rent a house and completely provide for himself. Daniel met Juan at a bar in L.A.'s Skid Row area one month after coming to Los Angeles. Juan helped him out of a tough situation, offered him a place to stay and basically rescued him from Skid Row streets for a short time. However, Daniel was not altogether happy cohabituating with Juan. Daniel says,

> I met him because I was in the bar . . . you know in the cantina. I had money right when I got here . . . the first time to Los Angeles. I had some money like forty, fifty dollars and I went to the bar and drink some beers. I don't know him. I was young and I see the security and they grab me like this. Juan saw me that I was young right and he talk to me. And he said, "Do you want to come to my house? Because I don't want to leave you in the street. Because you're drunk and I don't want people to rob you." He took me to his house and when I woke up in the morning I talked to him. He was gay. I had a relationship with him . . . like sex and all that.

Although he was apprehensive about engaging in homosexual relations with Juan, Daniel says that he slept with Juan because this assured him a place to stay, food and sometimes money. Despite their physical intimacy, Daniel never felt close to Juan and consequently, does not consider him a friend. He makes it clear that the physical relationship they shared was for him, only a means to securing shelter and other resources. According to Daniel, Juan knew that he was a reluctant sexual partner, primarily because he did not consider himself to be gay. Although, Daniel feels that his associate, Juan, took unfair advantage of his vulnerable situation, nevertheless, he offered him a temporary reprieve from the streets.

All too aware of existing power differentials and the exploitative capacity of some associates, some homeless men elect to maintain ties with even their least preferred associates in order to acquire resources like monetary loans, illicit drugs and even personal protection. Unlike Daniel, who was subjected to sexual exploitation by an associate, Deric (a homeless African American) continuously faces a perhaps less severe form of *financial* exploitation at the hand of his associates. Although he has a steady, good paying job at the University of Southern California Medical Center (County USC) his reliance on co-workers (associates) has actually made him more vulnerable to their economic exploitation:

> At work I may ask my supervisor to loan me money. That's about the only help I'll get. Sam . . . He's my main loan man. Sam and Willie! They play like they your friends but they ain't to . . . they suppose to be your friends but I'm not going to say they're my friends . . . both of them are supervisors. But Willie he's the supervisor over at General Relief. Sam he's the supervisor of all custodians. Both work there with me. [Refers to USC Hospital] I saw him [*Sam*] last night . . . saw Willie this morning! At night he's my supervisor [*Sam*], he tells me what to do and I go do it . . . but Willie, he works in the daytime. I see him when I be getting off of work, he be coming to work. He asked me if I needed money this morning. He was going to the bank about one o'clock today. I told him I'll talk to him Tuesday . . . get the money from him Tuesday that was all. Willie lend me fifty dollars Monday, I have to give him one hundred back! Payday was Friday. If I borrow fifty dollars I pay a hundred back, if I borrow a hundred I pay two hundred back.

Deric is caught in a revolving loan predicament with his associates at work. Even his co-workers say he makes too much money to live on the streets the way he does, yet his earnings are spent before he receives his next paycheck. Essentially, Deric pays his work associates 100 percent interest on the personal loans they make him, therefore he is constantly overdrawn even though every Friday is payday. These relationships are not based on genuine regard they have a strong profit motif for Deric's associates, who stand to double a portion of their income at Deric's expense. Deric is very aware of the conditions surrounding his association with Sam and Willie and he refuses to call them his friends simply because they present a friendly facade. Aside from his associates at work, Deric has only one other person he can borrow money from. This friend, Curtis, stands in sharp contrast to his co-workers. Unfortunately, Curtis is also homeless and seldom has any money to loan Deric. Unlike his work associates, loans among these friends are interest free. They have a friendly exchange of money and additional resources. Deric says,

> He looks out for me, I look out for him . . . I need money, he got I can get it. Tuesday night he was hungry, I gave him five dollars to go get him something to eat.

As evidenced above, both African Americans (as in Deric's case) and Americanized Latinos (Daniel's case) homeless men with limited social networks for securing resources choose to enter into exploitative relationships with associates out of sheer necessity.

Conflicting Expectations: Values and Roles

Outside of the realm of friendships, perhaps associates fail to develop closer relations due to conflicting values and role expectations. Through minimal interactions individuals form more continuous, deliberate relationships; however, affect (emotional attachment) and affinity (value congruency) are fundamental to the development of friendships (Rubin 1973; Lazarfeld and Merton 1954). Further, people's value orientations have an impact on their role expectations, which when conflicting can inhibit their interpersonal relationships. Such value conflicts are visibly stifling the relationship of two African American homeless men, Ron and Bobby. Ron has been episodically homeless for past four years and while he peddles merchandise around Skid Row to earn money his associate, Bobby, panhandles for a living, which Ron finds demeaning. Aside from Ron's distaste for panhandling, he does not feel that Bobby would provide him with much of anything, not food and certainly not money. Although, Ron and Bobby do relate as fellow street hustlers, pushing petty goods around downtown, their views on what are the appropriate means for surviving homelessness differ. Ron describes his relationship with Bobby as follows:

> Not really good . . . I mean not really close at all. He's a hustler like me. He always keeps things going too, you know. Same way like how I do. He always has something to sell to keep money in his pocket . . . and hustles. But he panhandles . . . he goes asks people for money. That's the only difference and I don't really like that. I mean . . . I'm poor and homeless, but I still got decency and respect. I like to earn my keep, you know . . . or whatever.

Ron and Bobby define their homeless situation and in turn, their individual roles distinctly. They base their role identifications on personal values and assessments of how to survive life on the streets. Consequently, conflicting role expectations keep Ron and Bobby from cultivating deeper ties. For one man panhandling is just another means for survival, while for the other it represents a lack of decency and self respect. They relate as homeless men, hustling merchandise in Skid Row and part ways where the practice of panhandling and what it represents is concerned.

The Illegal Social Scene

Skid row street life is saturated with illegal, income generating activity. Homeless men do what they can to survive—selling stolen merchandise, food stamps, sexual favors, and illegal drugs. Luis (a recent-immigrant from Mexico) sells illegal drugs in Skid Row for two of his housed and well-to-do associates. Luis' complicity notwithstanding, this situation is yet another example of how homeless men allow and endure their own exploitation at the hands of associates. Basically, Luis associates with two brothers that make a profit by investing money into buying drugs for Luis to sell in downtown L.A. Luis is certainly no "innocent" in this drug dealing arrangement he has going with these associates, however, he points out sarcastically that their relationships are out of convenience only. He makes "easy money" for these associates and in turn, they provide him with the opportunity to earn hundreds of dollars in an environment where few earn even minimum wage for a day's work. Luis says that he can either work for these associates, dealing the illegal drugs that subsidize their middle-class life-style, or he can work for the exploitative merchants in Skid Row and currently he opts for the former until he finds a good job. The relationships between Luis and his associates are purely opportunistic and as Luis says, "Si me quemaran," (if they burned him) during one of their drug deals he would have nothing more to do with them. Not all relationships among homeless men and their associates are as blatantly exploitative. In fact, most homeless men who experienced such exploitation were involved in asymmetrical power relations with the housed individuals, whereas, among homeless associates resources were exchanged casually and with greater equity.

SOCIAL CLUSTERS

At first glance, instances where long term ties exist among homeless men and their associates might signal the presence of meaningful relations, nonetheless, the focal point of such linkages is predominantly utilitarian. An important feature of friendships is that they engender a keenly emotional interpersonal dynamic, which when present among associates is typically secondary to their resource exchange preoccupations. Associates spend their leisure time just hanging out or rallying into groups, or social clusters, in order to take up collections for the purchase of alcohol or illegal drugs. Also, associates form social clusters to insure their personal safety, particularly at night. Although, they exhibit mutual concern for each other's personal safety (enough to warrant grouping for protection) their feelings for one another, while meaningful, remain quite superficial. A forty-nine year old, African American man, Jim, relates his experiences with his long time associates:

> We have a relationship to where we be on the street. We do drink, we drink together . . . daily! [Laughs] As a matter of fact, when I leave here we'll probably

go to Central Market and get some food, some roast beef and buy us a big forty ounce. Drink . . . shoot the shit, maybe buy us a joint of weed. Smoke a stick of marijuana.

We usually mingle together, me and Kenny and Ben and Ron. Protection, from the gang bangers! We got kind of a unity thing. We don't take much shit from the youngsters. We get our respect from them because you know we stick together and help each other in case of a little violence. We'll get rid of them. They know we don't bull shit. They can't rob us or jump us or take advantage of us because we're older guys right. We're considered the "O.G's," which would be original gangsters. We get our respect from them, they know we stick together.

Having known these men over ten years and seeing them regularly (three to four times a week), has not deepened Jim's esteem for them. As he puts it, "It's all basically a . . . street relationships." He is comfortable asking them for a couple of bucks or to accompany him while he goes about town collecting cans. In Jim's words they are "kind of a clique," and he contacts them by going "off down in the pits, down in Skid Row." At night they camp out together. Kenny and Ron have "girls" they sleep with, Jim and Ben go stag. As far as helping each other out, Jim says:

There's really not much that I would be needing that I could ask them for. Because they're basically in the same situation I am in. The only thing that I would be dependent on them for would be to get somebody off my ass or something like that. Finances? . . . You know if I'm going to jail, they couldn't help me get out of jail or something like that or with transportation somewhere. And you know housing, they couldn't put me up.

COERCIVE RELATIONS

In the extreme, the utilitarian-based nature of associate-type bonds leads to continuously coercive relations. Such mutual associates, then, maintain relations not because they want to but because they feel pressured to do so. In one such case, a twenty-four year old, Americanized Latino man continues to reluctantly remain in contact with the members of his old street gang—his "homeboys." Julian became homeless at age twenty-two, since which he has stayed periodically with some of his homeboys, even though he thinks of himself as an ex-gang member and feels little affection for gang members. His affiliation to these gang members dates back to his high school days, during which he was an active member of the gang. In the last couple of years since becoming homeless, Julian has tried to gradually distance himself from these homeboys. As Julian says,

I didn't hang around because I needed to or I wanted to but because I had to. If I quit them or something they'll come back and sweep me. Whatever I do . . . like even if I get a job throwing papers in the morning, sometimes I do that . . . go to work as a paper boy. I have to share my money with them. Sometimes they share their money with me, but not in the way that . . . Hey, I'm gonna give you this or that . . . no. They probably would go to the liquor store and buy some beer or whatever. Things like that . . . sometimes we go to restaurants, who ever has the money buys the food. We hang out together but after the night comes everybody goes their own way.

When hanging out with his homeboys, Julian prefers to have his own money and not depend on them because he says they are not his friends. Around his homeboys, all Julian has to do is say he is hungry and they take him out to eat. Yet in order to "hang out" with them he must have something to contribute as well, whether it is money, alcohol or other drugs. As Julian says the bottom line is, "You have to give to get." He describes the relationships among gang members generally as more contentious than agreeable. Julian's relationship with his homeboys resembles acquaintance-type linkages more closely than friendship-types, except the gang requires that its members protect each other regardless of whether they actually like each other.

Associates are not necessarily disingenuous relationships. Unlike friendships, associates are simply driven by a more pragmatic need fulfillment and low to moderate levels of emotional attachment. Friends are more apt to offer emotional and tangible assistance to their comrades, however, reciprocity in exchanging resources is equally as important in preserving relations with associates as it is among friends. Expecting to get "something for nothing" is simply not functional among homeless men. For most homeless men interviewed, a failure to reciprocate leads to feelings of disrespect, distrust, irresponsibility and contempt. Because these affiliations are more instrumental than expressive in function, the extent of tangible exchanges among ties is the primary criteria by which these relations are evaluated and not their mutual intimacy or commitment (as is common among friendship links). In a world where material resources are scarce, relationships keenly geared toward exchange functions are valuable to the survival of homeless people.

Summary

In the previous chapter we examined the social networks of homeless men with regard to their form and functions (network variables), while, this chapter has focused on the substantive context of the social relations found within network structures (relational/link variables). In order to show that even the most tenuous of ties among homeless men play a meaningful role in their survival, I have taken a close look at the relational attributes of their links to casual acquaintances and to associates. Also examined, was the social context or homeless social milieu within which such relations are formed or maintained. Ethnic differences and/or similarities were noted throughout the examination.

Substantively, the analysis of the relational aspects of social networks revealed that even the weak or tenuous ties (casual acquaintance and associates) of homeless men facilitate their survival by: 1) providing for the circulation of useful information throughout their environment; 2) identifying them, to some extent, as insiders within the social world of homeless people; 3) providing them with a measure of anonymity by trivializing the use of individual names; 4) providing tangible resources; 5) maintaining flexible or loosely knit relations, with few normative or behavioral expectations; 6) maintaining the norm of reciprocity by either tangible (e.g., monetary, food, alcohol exchanges) or latent (e.g., moral support or companionship in exchange for a beer) means; and 7) maintaining a highly instrumental rather than expressive relational disposition, thereby, concentrating on useful exchange functions. We have also seen that, along with benefits, these weak links carry some liabilities as well. For instance, the incidental nature of life on the streets and the imposing organizational structures of many shelters and meal facilities generate incidental interactions among homeless individuals—making it difficult to for them to develop closer relations. The lack of social intimacy among many homeless men tends to turn their focus toward the compensatory aspects of their relations, which can result in even more fragile and tentative linkages. Along these lines, asymmetrical power relations may develop, leading affiliates into exploitative exchanges. Conflicting normative expectations may also impede the formation of more enduring ties, and in extreme cases, coercive relations may eventually terminate further interactions. Nevertheless, the saliency of weak ties is evident given their highly instrumental capacity and strategic ingenuity in filling the survival gap left by social service providers. In the following chapter we shall see how more enduring relations, friendships, also sustain homeless men in their endeavors to survive homelessness.

Chapter Five

Getting by with a
Little Help from Their Friends

If the social milieu of homeless individuals consisted only of casual relations (i.e., acquaintances and associates), then based on the descriptions offered in the previous chapter we could conclude that these men exist in a state of emotional isolation; that is, lacking intimate interpersonal bonds. Fortunately, most homeless Latinos and African Americans report having at least one close friend they can count on for support. And although much has been made of the apparent conviviality and tenuous nature of their relationships (Rossi 1989; Snow and Anderson 1993), to focus on this alone obscures the complex network of social relations engaged by homeless men. Again, their ties range from interactions with vast numbers of casual acquaintances, to a smaller yet instrumental number of associates, to more socially intimate friendships. Thus, they exhibit what one anthropologist referred to as "marginality without isolation" (Lovell 1984).

Substantively this chapter is the outcome of inquiries into how homeless men initiate and maintain friendship linkages (as distinguished from casual acquaintances and associates). Moreover, Latino and African American men were asked, "How many friends can you count on for help?" They sometimes responded, "What do mean by friends?" Interviewers then followed-up with, "Whatever friendship means to you." At which point we usually received clarification of who did and did not rank among their friends. Variations exist in the nature of friendships homeless men maintain, however, the minimum criteria through which they identify their friends is as follows: 1) there is a genuinely strong feeling of social intimacy, affection and concern; 2) such ties are well established, usually for a period of several years; 3) they are regarded as trustworthy companions; and 4) they engage in a reciprocal exchange of valued resources.

While, poets, idealists and even greeting card writers may romantically proclaim that friends are not made—they're born, more often than not friendships are deliberately constructed through ongoing interaction. Usually, friendships emerge within a specific social context and among individuals sharing a similar social position (Jackson 1977). Still, friendships are notably special social relations. They are also among the most voluntary and intimate relationships cultivated by individuals (Jackson 1977) and the friendships of homeless men are no exception. Whether forged prior to or during their homeless crisis, for these men friendships are special relations that are distinguished from less intimate ties.

Aside from the emotional attachments or even the commonality of values that ignite many friendships, social network analyst remind us of the exchange components present in such relations (Toohey, et. al. 2004; Jackson 1977). That is, implicit components such as social intimacy and explicit components involving the services or resources that are provided through such ties. From the network perspective friendships are seen primarily as exchanges having implied costs and benefits. To the extent that friendships provide resources (e.g., food, financial help or just someone to talk to), they are beneficial. And their costs lie in the efforts individuals expend to maintain these relationships (e.g., personal time or monetary investments in the relationship). Essentially, this suggests that enduring friendships are the product of equitable resource exchanges among participants. Moreover, unbalanced resource exchanges foster individual power differentials that can adversely impact relationships (Lin 2001). Such exchange requisites are particularly problematic among homeless men, who by definition have few tangible resources to share with friends.

FACTORS IMPACTING FRIENDSHIP AMONG HOMELESS MEN

In attempting to understand the importance of friendships in the social networks of homeless men, several factors were discerned. Table 5.1 presents these factors, each of which are elaborated on below and further illustrated through the perspectives of homeless men. Some of these factors are specifically highlighted in the chapter by section subheading, while others are discussed throughout. Moreover, table 5.1 charts the factors and conditions that impact the development and maintenance of friendship bonds for homeless men. The table begins by noting the distinct contextual character of friendships established prior to the onset of homelessness, pre-homeless relations, compared those acquired after becoming homeless, homeless relations.

Table 5.1.   Factors Impacting Friendship among Homeless Men

	Pre-Homeless Relations*	*Homeless Relations***
Social Intimacy	Highly Expressive Instrumental	Expressive Instrumental
Social Context	School Work Neighborhood Home Town/Country Military	Street Encampments Shelters Meal Facilities Detox Programs Service Agencies Day Labor Shadow Work
Exchange Capacity	Financial Temporary Shelter Meals/Subsistence	Limited Financial Frequent-Companionship Protection Meals/Subsistence Alcohol, Cigarettes, Small goods Information
Power Differentials	Asymmetrical	Symmetrical
Role Identification	Ethnicity SES Homie Military Buddies Co-Workers Family Roles	Ethnicity Day Laborer Truck Lumper Social Buddies *Paisanos* Street Buddies
Reciprocity	Latent Unequal	Latent More Equitable

Notes:
*Refers to friendships established prior to becoming homeless.
**Refers to friendships acquired after becoming homeless.

Simple longevity indicates that pre-homeless relations/friendships tend to be more enduring linkages than are homeless relations/friendships, because they have usually existed well before individuals first experience homelessness. These contextual categories set the scene within which homeless men play out their friendships—either by linking them to more conventionally based interactions with housed individuals and/or to subcultural interactions with their homeless compeers.

Within each contextual base (pre-homeless or homeless relations), social intimacy is a key factor defining their friendship bonds (refer to table 5.1). Among homeless men friendships tend to be expressively oriented, that is, as opposed to instrumentally oriented ties that focus on successive tangible exchanges, these linkages function primarily through an exchange of emotional or moral support engendering feelings of affection, trust and loyalty (MacK-nee and Mervyn 2002; Bao, et. al. 2000). Nevertheless, given their expressive component, the friendships of homeless men also prove instrumental in providing tangible assistance. Although homeless men can indeed count on their friends for help, these bonds are so notably intimate that unlike their more casual relationships (i.e., acquaintances and associates), they are sustained even when few material resources are exchanged. Thus, while all relationships have a varying instrumental function, friendships (as defined by homeless men) also require expressions of social intimacy.

Furthermore, all relationships take shape within a particular social context that binds and defines the nature of one's personal ties. In the case of homeless men, many of their pre-homeless friendships develop in typical settings such as schools; work environments; old neighborhoods; their home town or homeland; and even within military settings. In stark contrast, their homeless friendships emerge through nightly encounters at street encampments, at shelters, meal facilities, detoxification programs and other social service agencies. These friendships also develop in the course of earning an income. For instance, their friendships unfold while seeking work as day laborers, or generally engaging in unconventional forms of opportunistic and innovative shadow work (Snow and Anderson 1993)—that is, while taking on odd jobs around Skid Row like panhandling for money, or recycling items for profit. In a nutshell, the development of homeless friendships occurs within the balance of a subcultural street life, which by definition provides an unstable context for initiating and pursuing friendships that are inarguably vital to the lives of these men.

A further word is needed on shelter and other service providers that assist homeless people. Unfortunately the organizational structure of many emergency facilities often discourage the maintenance of friendships among homeless individuals and thus, disregard the functional and emotional significance that such relationships have for these men. Disrupting the relationships of homeless men hampers their efforts to regain self-sufficiency, given the repertoire of interpersonal survival strategies infused within such relationships. Men seeking the assistance of service providers must leave their personal roles outside the shelter doors. Often the administration of homeless shelters operate with such institutional vigor that rules adopted to regulate individual conduct produce conflicts between the personal and shelter roles of their homeless clients (Stark 1994). Service providers employ mechanisms that enable them to exert control over their organizational environment, thus, program or in residence affiliations with such agencies usually result in limited or completely broken homeless, peer relationships (Snow and Anderson 1993). Shelter residents are obliged to accommodate house rules and policies,

which highly structure their daily routines by either leaving no time for socializing with street friends or frowning on it.

The exchange capacity of their relationships varies depending on whether
these are pre-homeless or homeless friendships. As previously stated, while
friendships offer material resources they are more clearly defined by their
emotional attachment and interpersonal commitments. Yet, the capacity for
material exchange is an important function of friendship and equity in resource exchange depends on the equality of social positions. Since homeless
men have few tangible resources and occupy a low social position, they have
a low capacity for exchange (Hurlbert, et. al. 2000). This exchange disparity
becomes more pronounced when we examine the exchange capacity of their
pre-homeless relationships (who tend to be housed individuals) compared to
that of their homeless relationships (most of whom are also homeless).

Most of their pre-homeless relations (table 5.1, see exchange capacity) can
and have provided these men with temporary shelter, financial help in the
form of moderate monetary gifts and/or loans, meals, and overall, help them
meet a variety of subsistence needs (i.e., providing a place to wash up, store
their belongings or providing clothing, blankets, shoes . . . etc.). Friendships
acquired during their homelessness (homeless relations, table 5.1) tend to be
with homeless compeers, who unable to provide many of the afore mentioned
resources—instead offer a myriad of humble services and items such as: limited financial help (e.g., small monetary loans or gifts); companionship and
protection at night-time encampments and shelters; exchange of meals (subsistence needs), alcohol, cigarettes and other small goods; and they exchange
of information on available services and income sources. Mutual survival becomes an important dynamic of these relationships, because each is well
aware of the crisis they face and as friends, they do what they can for each
other. However, homeless men tend to place a premium on social intimacy
and not the exchange capacity of their friendships. Still, patterns of unilateral
exchanges (or limited reciprocity, to be discussed shortly) produce power differentials in their relations. Moreover, their unequal social status and scarce
resources place them in asymmetrical relationships, particularly with housed
individuals. The impact of power differentials among friends is sometimes
countered by their role identification. How they see themselves and significant others will affect the nature of their behavior toward each other. For
instance, some pre-homeless friends share identifiers such as: ethnicity; so-
cial-economic status; "old homie" (from their old neighborhood); military
buddies; old co-workers; and also acknowledge their pre-homeless roles as
family members (brothers, fathers or husbands). While, homeless friends
share role identifiers relating to their survival activities such as: day laborers;
truck lumpers; buddies; and paisanos (countrymen sharing a similar U.S.

immigrant experience); and as night time street buddies (meeting up on the streets and at night encampments).

Another important dynamic of friendship among homeless men, involves the willingness of individuals to provide each other with reciprocal assistance. Reciprocity among these friends is based less on manifested exchanges of tangible resources, concentrating instead on the latent understanding that if possible most types of assistance would gladly be given—this is the case for relationships acquired both prior to homelessness (pre-homeless) and during homelessness (homeless). However, the meaning and burden of reciprocity changes based on how relationships are defined (i.e., acquaintance, associate or friendship). As chapter four indicates, linkages with acquaintances and particularly with associates must produce tangible reciprocity if these relationships are to continue. However, the issue of reciprocity among friends is very different. Inability to equitably compensate friends for their support leaves homeless men expressing personal sentiments of shame, sadness and disappointment. Further, their attachment to friends remains even with infrequent contact and few exchanges. As table 5.1 indicates, given the differing social position and limited frequency of contact or companionship existing among pre-homeless friends (i.e., pre-homeless relations particularly among housed and homeless individuals), their resource exchanges tend to be inequitable compared to the incidents of exchange reported among friends who are both homeless (homeless relations).

CASE STUDY OF FRIENDSHIP NETWORKS: LATINO AND AFRICAN AMERICAN MEN

Social networks play a crucial role in linking homeless men to opportunities and resources. Friendships as a component of this complex mesh of social relations are equipped to confer emotional, as well as material benefits to recipients. And while friendships are intimately regarded linkages they are, nevertheless, impacted by various constraining and yielding factors (i.e., those highlighted in table 5.1). These are also contextually based linkages that by their association assign homeless men meaningful identities that extend beyond homeless roles. In fact, through their ties to friends, and other individuals, these men exercise social networking options that facilitate their daily survival.

What follows is a case study analysis, examining how homeless men enlist the help of friends in making sense of their lives on the streets. The hope here is, that by examining their personal accounts we can better understand the active, interpretive and constructive capacities employed by homeless men in negotiating their social world. The social networking practices (involving friendships) of Latinos (both Americanized and recent-immigrant) and African Americans are analyzed with an overall focus on the saliency of their friendship bonds. Furthermore, factors impacting their friendship linkages (listed in table 5.1) are highlighted by section subheading and discussed in detail.

Social Intimacy

Not only do homeless individuals benefit from establishing friendships, but the unique saliency of this bond is expressed by their selective reference to others as friends. James (a homeless African American man), has four friends that provide him with much needed companionship and monetary support. While their support serves him well, he is guarded about striking up new friendships and makes it clear that in this environment there are only a few people he can trust:

> Due to the situation, the environment that I'm involved with right now . . . There's not a lot of people out here that you can trust, that you can call friends. You have to be very selective because the majority of the people down here will sell you out or take from you . . . or set you up to be ripped off by somebody bigger than shit! This is the only thing they think about is how can I get this next hit of dope. How can I hustle this, or can I borrow this money . . . if they can't borrow it, they'll find a way to take it from you.

The Skid Row environment is a place where the "destitute" congregate in hopes of receiving a meal or bed for the night. Among these individuals, approximately half are thought to have substance abuse problems (Koegel, et. al.1995). This combination of concentrated poverty and drug abuse breeds an environment with great potential for crime, and homeless individuals are rightly cautious. When we note that in 1984 over 10,000 homeless individuals were concentrated in Los Angeles' downtown area (HUD 1984; Farr 1984), and increasing to estimates as high as 42,000 homeless during 1994 (Shelter Partnership 1995) and to 80,000 in the County of Los Angeles by 2000 (Los Angeles Homeless Services Authority 2003)—is it any wonder that homeless men like James, are wary of life on these streets and suspicious of the intentions of others! People who rank as friends among homeless men have earned this distinction by displaying trustworthiness, affection, some kind of reciprocal assistance and overall camaraderie. James further highlights the necessary elements defining his friendships, in discussing his relationship with Aaron:

> We're very tight. He draws unemployment insurance also and I can borrow money from him. In turn, when my check comes in I pay him back and loan him

money as well. We pretty much hang out together, during the daytime. We just walk around and converse, talk about the situation that we're in and stuff and what he wants to do . . . Aaron really wants a job real bad, he wants to get back into the work force. And just talk about things in general. How we can improve ourselves. We pretty much look out for each other. That comes with trust; you have to build that trust.

As illustrated by James' relationship with Aaron (who is also homeless), close friendships that are endowed with a mutual exchange of resources, companionship, protection and trust are assets for surviving out on the streets. African American homeless men routinely rely on the support of friends, calling on each other almost daily—thus, testing the durability of their relationships. These friendships provide what service agencies and relatives cannot—they take the edge off their crisis by seeing them through the recurring rough and penniless points in their lives. Most importantly, elements of trust and affection within their friendships are established over time and, given their homeless situation, very much appreciated.

For African American men participating in this study these linkages were among the more consistent and enduring relationships in their lives, most reported knowing friends for at least a decade. Many researchers (Rossi 1989; Cohen and Sokolovsky 1989; Snow and Anderson 1993) have noted the tenuous, utilitarian and seemingly shallow nature of relationships among homeless men, and while this may accurately describe some of their relations, friendships are an altogether different matter. Friendships among these Skid Row dwellers are selectively developed and usually established long ago. This indicates that at least some of their non-kin affiliations are motivated by more than simply a compensatory function. Acquaintances and perhaps associates may be casually and quickly acquired ties, but even among the homeless friendships involve meaningful interactions and long-term exchanges. Homeless for more than eight years, Jim (African American) discussed the reasons he considers Mike his friend:

Times when I'm real down, real dire situation . . . I can depend on Mike. I'll go and we'll rap. We'll have conversations and he'll give me two or three dollars or sometimes he'll give me twenty bucks, if I really need it. Sometimes he'll see me pushing my basket down the street and he'll stop me and give me some change. Situations like that. Sometimes he'll a . . . he's got this car and we'll ride around and talk . . . about Kenny! [Laughs] Me and Mike we're something like brothers.

Jim and Mike have been friends for fourteen years, during which time they have witnessed each others homeless episodes. Although Mike is currently employed and has his own place, Jim consistently sees him twice a week.

Their relationship is anything but trivial, it is purposeful and gratifying. In his opening statement, Jim portrays Mike as someone he can count on when things are really down and dire. Clearly Mike offers Jim material aid and companionship, but more importantly, even when not solicited his help is freely given whenever he sees the need. The intensity of his attachment to Mike runs so deep that Jim likens him to a brother. Simply put, Jim says, "We've got a beautiful relationship." In Skid Row, sentiments run deep among many homeless men who regularly characterized the intimacy of their friendships with familial adjectives such as, "like a sister," "brother close" or "father like." For homeless men like Jim, close friends commonly become surrogate family members. Moreover, they construct kin-like bonds with a few select non-kin relations and therefore, retain a sense of belonging and feel supported by people who care.

While Latinos maintain less contact with their friends than African Americans, their friendships are also distinguished by a high level of social intimacy, trust and mutual support. Latino friendships usually are not spur of the moment relationships prompted by a couple of drinks on a cold night— although, certainly some enduring friendships among homeless and housed people alike may begin in just this way. Rather, Latino friendships tend to be linkages established prior to their homeless crisis, commonly existing for a period of several years and as long as nine years (Americanized and recent-immigrant Latinos, respectively). Lucas (a Spanish speaking, long-term U.S. resident from Mexico), who has been periodically homeless for more than ten years considers himself fortunate to count Martin among his friends[1]:

> Well, I consider him because he had offered me many times . . . he has offered me his home, because he is married. Sometimes when he sees me like this without work, many times he has offered me money. And well, he has told me that when I need a favor or something, to turn to him. For this I consider him my friend.

Lucas has known Martin for only two years but he relates to him as if he were his childhood friend. Lucas was first introduced to Martin (who is now his closest friend) by some of his mutual acquaintances who he has known for over ten years. During their short tenure as friends, Martin has proved to be a valued friend to Lucas by consistently showing his affection, support and concern for Lucas' well-being. Martin, a housed friend, is quick to offer Lucas any kind of support he can. Yet, Lucas feels ashamed of his situation and shies away from Martin's supportive gestures. Lucas avoids his friend's well intentioned charity because it is an obvious indicator to him of his impoverished state, and low social status. Still, his bout with homelessness does not keep Lucas from continually socializing with his friend Martin, on the weekends at the local park. In fact, these recreational encounters shift the focus away from his homelessness and onto his identity as friend. Hence, minimizing the asymmetrical power distribution among these friends and giving Lucas' life a semblance of normalcy.

Social Context: Ethnicity

How do homeless Latinos compare to their African American counterparts in regards to their background and their friends? To understand the relevance of friendships in the lives of homeless men, we must consider the interaction of ethnicity (or race) along with social structural factors (e.g., economic, employment and educational opportunities) in shaping these ties. That is, the full ethnic social context within which friendships emerge requires our attention. For instance, census data reveals most residents of urban ghettos were largely African American or Latino (McKinnon 2003; Ramirez and de la Cruz 2002). The high representation of minorities within inner-city neighborhoods is troubling because these areas hold few opportunities for social mobility. Residents here suffer from the effects of persistent joblessness, inadequate job hunting networks, and poor schools (Wilson 1996). The economic and social marginality of today's urban ghetto weighs so heavily on its residents that it has become a place of chronic subordination. About the imposing social structural forces that impact the lives of residents in the ghetto, Wilson says (1996:52):

> . . . [edited] it is important to understand and communicate the overwhelming obstacles that many ghetto residents have to overcome just to live up to mainstream expectations involving work, the family and the law. Such expectations are taken for granted in middle-class society. Americans in more affluent areas have jobs that offer fringe benefits; they are accustomed to health insurance that covers paid sick leave and medical care. They do not live in neighborhoods where attempts at normal child-rearing are constantly undermined by social forces that interfere with healthy child development. And their families' prospects for survival do not require at least some participation in the informal economy (that is, an economy in which income is unreported and therefore not taxable).

The rise in American homelessness is just one of the many unhealthy social ramifications of larger constraining structural forces. However, Wilson (1996:55) does caution:

> This is not to argue that individuals and groups lack the freedom to make their own choices, engage in certain conduct, and develop certain styles and orienta-

tions, but it is to say that these decisions and actions occur within a context of constraints and opportunities that are drastically different from those present in middle-class society.

Therefore, returning to our focus on friendships among homeless Latino and African American men, it is important to note that most of these bonds develop and exist within the adverse social context of life in the urban ghetto.

Still, as noted earlier friendships are definitely distinctive, more intimate, linkages among homeless individuals and given the extreme impoverishment of these men it becomes doubly interesting to examine exactly who their friends are. In this respect, several questions arise, for instance, "Were these friendship forged prior to or during the onset of homelessness?" "How do homeless men initiate and maintain such ties given their situation?" And, "Are there ethnic differences among homeless men in the formation and maintenance of friendships?"

Based on the vignettes presented below we see that some individuals initiate friendships during the course of their homelessness, particularly those who are among the long-term or "chronic" homeless, other men maintain friendships established during 'better times', and still others are surprised to meet up with their old high school friends who have also become Skid Row dwellers. Mark (an African American man) has been homeless nine years and never expected to see his high school sweet heart down and out in Skid Row:

> We been knowing each other since high school. When I found out she was downtown pushing baskets it kind of like . . . hurt me. Because she . . . we graduated! Irene was in a class of females that was going to do better in life. All of a sudden I found out she was downtown pushing baskets, it kind of shocked me.

Lately, Mark sees Irene almost everyday because she is staying at the same shelter. Irene is now the girlfriend of his best friend Louis, who is also homeless and staying at the Dome Village shelter located on the outskirts of down town Los Angeles' business district (run by Ted Hayes, a strong advocate for homeless people). Moreover, most homeless African American participants in this study have homeless friends that they know since their high school days. On the one hand, like Mark, domiciled people might feel astonished at the sight of one of their old school friends wandering through the streets, homeless. On the other hand, the chances of having homeless high school friends may increase with the level of socio-economic deprivation experienced within one's old neighborhood.

In examining how homeless Latinos compare to their African American compeers, keep in mind that we are looking here at two Latino groups that, by nature of their respective cultural and U.S. resident status, are differentially integrated into the social and economic fabric of American life. Homeless Latinos that are native-born or are Americanized speaking long-term residents are more assimilated into American society and thus, are experientially similar to homeless African Americans compared with the recent-immigrant Latinos in this study (who are discussed in the next section). Moreover, given their oftentimes low economic means many of these Americanized Latinos are also inevitably affected by the same structurally fashioned poverty traps (i.e., the educational, employment and economic opportunity constraints) that afflict other inner-city residents (e.g., African Americans).

Within this bleak socio-economic context, for Martin (an English speaking, long-term U.S. resident from Puerto Rico), was able to salvage one of his pre-homeless friendships. Martin has known Linda for fifteen years, she has been a friend to both he and his estranged wife. Despite his homeless crisis he has kept his relationship with Linda on good terms. Although, his change in status does weigh on their relations, as he recounts they are close and:

> Very friendly . . . no inhibitions. We will talk like we were brothers and sisters. She has an office in Huntington Park and no matter who was in the office, when I went . . . no matter how dirty I was, how in bad shape I looked, she always welcomed me, invited me into her office. She didn't ask me if I needed money, she would just give me money . . . ten, twenty dollars. That was anytime I went to see her. For me that was . . . I consider that a friend. The relationship was strained. After a while I stopped going. It was getting to be embarrassing for both of us.

Martin's description conveys elements of affection, concern and respect present in his friendship with Linda, elements that are important in most meaningful relationships. Social intimacy notwithstanding, the remnants of past relations between Martin and Linda were not enough to counter the effects of their now markedly different social positions. Relations between housed and homeless people, inevitably suffer the strain of financial inequities and interpersonal power differentials. Often, these once meaningful and reciprocated friendships are besieged by currents of emotions that take negative and deteriorating directions. Homeless men are no longer able to entertain friends in their homes, can offer few material resources, and their poverty inspires the sympathy of people who were once their equals. Consequently, friends who related to one another's lifestyle may imagine but cannot share in the other's experience. Homeless individuals are far removed from the daily routine of conventionally housed individuals and housed individuals can never fully understand what it means to live out on the streets with only temporary shelter.

At its core, homelessness is a reification of the broader socio-economic structures of poverty: poor educational opportunities; low skill levels; joblessness; and the deficit of low-income housing (Rossi 1989; Wright 1989). The real shock lies in finding that many of these homeless men come from each other's old neighborhoods and not from some untimely industrial plant closure in middle-class, America as some well meaning advocates for the homeless would have us believe. A response to the question, "How many of your old friends are homeless?" might well be contingent on the socio-economic status of one's parents. Almost by social structural design (particularly, the limited availability of affordable housing nationwide), impoverished inner-city people are more apt to be among the prospectively homeless citizenry (Shinn and Gillespie 1994).

At first glance, the "Latino paradox of high poverty and low rates of homelessness" (Gonzalez-Baker 1994:491) might seem to contradict a structural causation explanation of homelessness. However, a closer look reveals that for Latinos, cultural support patterns may mitigate the effects of poverty and therefore, the onset of homelessness (Burt 1992; Gonzalez-Baker 1994). Specifically with regard to housing, Latinos are more likely than African Americans to enter into residential arrangements that involve overcrowding, adult children living with parents, and multiple families in a single home (for an extensive discussion see Gonzalez-Baker 1994). On the issue of structural poverty and homelessness, Susan Gonzalez-Baker (1994:498) concludes that, "Latino social support seems to be more likely to include diverse housing arrangements within the interpersonal network as a strategy for avoiding life on the streets in the face of persistent poverty." Further commenting on the under-representation of Latinos among the homeless (relative to their population size) Gonzalez-Baker states (1994:498), ". . . the Latino paradox can be explained in large measure by the particular way in which Latino populations have adapted to their constrained opportunity structure by sharing housing as a material resource more frequently and in more varied ways than may be true of other ethnic groups."

Turning our attention to homeless recent-immigrant Latinos, we find that their situation of homelessness is fundamentally different from their more Americanized counterparts (e.g., English speaking Latinos and African Americans). For many homeless recent immigrants or long-term residents, their poverty constraints are overshadowed by their immigrant "illegal" or "alien" resident status in the U.S. Their recent migration and/or their inability to speak English makes these homeless Latinos less socially integrated within American society. This lack of social integration then targets them for increased exploitation in the work force and in general compromises their human rights through increased discrimination within their host country (Chavez 1989). Many of these homeless Latinos find themselves unable to secure steady employment, even if the job is underpaid. And in part, fearing arrest and deportation they hesitate to stand in meal lines even when they are unable to provide a meal for themselves. Homeless long-term U.S. residents (Spanish speaking) are also finding it increasingly difficult to get a job and are constantly struggling with unfair wages, hours and work conditions.

However among homeless Latinos, it is recent immigrants that seem especially vulnerable given their undocumented status and their stated lack of familiarity with American organizations and institutions. Thus, these homeless Latinos find themselves struggling to minimize the degree of exploitation they face at the hands of local employers by working hard to prove their labor power in hopes of increasing their wages. This "hard working" strategy is rarely successful because employers hire homeless, undocumented Latinos precisely because they can profit by exploiting them—they are indeed a source of cheap labor to employers in Skid Row specifically and to U.S. employers generally (Chavez 1989).

Much of the literature on immigration tells us that migration chains facilitate the journey north for new immigrants by granting them a place of refuge in the U.S. and thereby, assisting them in their transition into American society (Massey, et. al. 1987). However, in the case of homeless, recent immigrants, traditional migration chains are unavailable to them because: 1) they have few relatives living in the U.S. to assist them; 2) they are estranged from these relatives; or 3) they simply have no family members in the U.S. with whom to link up. The lack of strong migration chains among recent waves of immigrants to the U.S. is not surprising (i.e., immigrants from Central America), but migration chains between Mexico and U.S. are long established and yet all homeless recent immigrants interviewed came from Mexico. One explanation for this occurrence is that the random selection process simply did not yield a sample of recently immigrated Central Americans dwelling in Skid Row—perhaps because of the larger pool of Mexican immigrants in the area. The alternate explanation is that these homeless recent immigrant participants are initiating Mexican-U.S. migration chains within their family circles, or they are venturing into new geographic regions where they have no prior migratory ties and thus, they end up homeless in America.

This is the social context within which homeless Latinos, both recent immigrants and Spanish speaking long-term residents, selectively interact with friends. Surely life out on L.A. streets is best when spent in the company of friends, however, between searching for jobs and their next meal these immigrants spend less time visiting or hanging out with friends compared to Americanized Latinos and African Americans. And while they have only a few friends they can turn to during especially rough times, their friendships are long standing and are typically with immigrants from their homeland. After becoming homeless for the first time at age thirty one, George (a Spanish speaking, long-term resident in the U.S. from Mexico) finds he has only one friend that he can still relate to because as he puts it[2]:

> Because, well. He is the only friend that I've had all my life. Because he . . . since eighteen years old, we've been around each other. Well, we used to be around each other . . . We came to this country and well, he got married here. He has his home and everything. And always when I need something, I turn to him. But not recently because his wife is very . . . she can't even see me, his wife.

George's account of meeting up with a childhood friend from his homeland while in the U.S. is commonly reiterated by other Spanish speaking homeless men. Although, George has resided in the U.S. for more than ten years, Alfonso (his long time friend) is the only person that he can trust and definitely the only friend who helps and supports him. George says that he loves Alfonso as deeply as he does his own brothers.

Similarly, homeless, Latinos that are recent immigrants also maintain enduring friendships with fellow immigrants. Recent immigrants are in a rather problematic situation because if they lack legal immigration documents they can be deported by the police and other authorities at any time, which means they must be particularly guarded about their social affiliations. During four of the last twelve months since he has resided in the U.S., an undocumented Latino man told me of the hardships he endures now that (for the first time in his life) he is without a home. When he first migrated to the U.S. Marcos found a steady job, which made it possible for him to relocate his wife to Los Angeles as well. Eight months later he lost his job, his wife had to return to Mexico and he has been homeless since then. While living in an apartment with his wife, Marcos did not socialize with any friends it was only after her departure that he happened on two of his hometown friends. This nineteen year old recent immigrant, Marcos (Spanish speaking), cautiously keeps to himself around Los Angeles yet he is not overly concerned about being deported back to Mexico. Marcos was fortunate to meet up with friends, he says:[3]

> It happened in an unforeseen way. Even though we came at different times [refers to migration to the U.S.A] But we ended up encountering each other, the three of us, by chance on Broadway. And well, they have known how to give me a hand until now. [Edited] We get along well. We try to rise above all the problems that exist between us. Communicate with each other about what is going on . . . well, sometimes they tell me about a job and I go verify if they still need someone or not. We go to the parks and spend some free time, like on Sundays. And like this . . . successively every weekend. [Trans.]

Marcos is a reserved, very proper and polite young man who's only telling teenage signs are his boyish face, a hand held portable cassette player and the headphones that dangle from his neck when not in use. Space permitting, Marcos spends the night at Dolores Mission (a shelter in East Los Angeles) where he limits his interaction with other shelter occupants to a little conversation and a few tips on job prospects. Encountering his friends, Samuel and Quiros, has proved rather fortunate as they help him financially, with food, a place to stay and especially emotionally as sounding boards for his problems and concerns. Without these two hometown friends, this homeless nineteen year old man would walk the streets of Los Angeles in complete isolation and with even fewer resources.

Social Context: Involving Relationships

Whether friendships emerge within the subcultural activity of Skid Row or within the social context of conventionally housed people—the existence of such intimate bonds among homeless men is a pleasant surprise. And while homeless affiliations vary in the level of support and self-validation they provide, with acquaintances and friendships on opposite ends of the continuum, the interpersonal saliency of these peer relationships is lost if we focus on their utilitarian qualities alone. Time and time again we have heard it said that, "A friend in need is a friend indeed." These words should be etched on Skid Row sidewalks where everyday the truly down and out do what they can to lend their friends a helping hand. Recognizing that friends, like material resources, are scarce when you are homeless, some African Americans (and Latinos) maintain strong emotional connections with their friends. Yes, their friends provide material assistance, but more so they provide emotional support and interpersonal self-validation. While close friendships exist among both African American men and among their homeless, recently immigrated Latino counterparts, the friendship networks of African American men are more extensive. Art, a forty-eight year old African American man, articulates the basis of his friendship with his closest friend, Buddy (who is also homeless):

> When we see each other going down hill or something . . . It's hard for a guy down here to talk to people, without getting a lot of bull shit. It's hard for me to talk to somebody and I can talk to him about a lot of things that are inside of me. Certain pains in me . . . I can't do that with everybody. It's emotional . . . [edited] . . . I can trust him. We've worked together for about four years and he's never done anything to harm me and I've never done anything to harm him. We share things. He's the type of guy that . . . when you're in the service, type of guy that you got to find . . . your one person that you can depend on. That you

can almost trust your life with. He's that type of guy. As far as friends, he's one of the guys that reminds me of the old time friends. We just get along good. You figure we've worked together everyday for four years; we've never had an argument. They say he and I are two of the best loaders in town. That causes a lot of jealousy and envy but he's my Buddy—that's my friend.

Companionship helps most of us combat isolation and loneliness and is essential to our emotional well-being and this is acutely true for homeless men. Art and Buddy hang out together throughout the day and often spend their nights sleeping near each other out on the streets. Homeless peers engaged in socially intimate bonds mutually negotiate their existence on Skid Row by acting as survival buddies. As the vignette above illustrates, homeless friends affirm their mutual self worth by validating one another's roles as friends, confidants, supporters and co-workers, that is, by asserting their identities beyond homeless labels and stigmas. To each other they are more than destitute people beholden to service providers and welfare agencies, they are people sharing a personal history and friendship with each other. These individuals knew each other when—when times were good, when they were children, and in some instances when they were economically self-sufficient. Some of their friendships have outlasted Reaganomics as well as the "kinder" and "gentler" presidency.

To be sure, homeless African Americans on Skid Row share more than just the lived experience of homelessness many have friendships that far predate their homeless status. Whether the bonds of friendship were forged through homelessness or during more prosperous days, homeless compeers bid each other what is typically unattainable from care givers—intimate levels of understanding, self-worth and validation of their multiple roles. Hearing Ray (an African American man) speak of his relationship with his friend Johnny, crystallizes the kind of personal histories and concerns that link many homeless men:

> He's an older fellow. Him, and I were friends back in the times when both of us were rather prosperous. And that kind of cements us together, by knowing where we came from. I've known Johnny for like, maybe thirty years. But now, see he's . . . he has a place of his own. It's a converted basement, but he's stable. To the degree as to where we can go and leave personal possessions that are valuable to us there and know that they're alright [edited] . . . Our relationship is really not based on the help that we can give each other. Like I say, our relationship is based upon the things that we know about life and we discuss them and it's just like . . . confirmation. You know, "Man did you see? Or, "Did you know?" We read the paper and we discuss events and where it looks like we're going . . . How he's doing and how I'm doing.

From Ray's personal outlook, we see the importance of self-validation or con-
firmation of their mutual values, attitudes and roles. Longevity in the friendship of these men has exposed them to good and bleak times and rather than
dissolving their relations it has solidified them.

Unlike, African Americans who maintain connections to well known
friends residing mostly in the Los Angeles area, the friendships of recent-immigrant Latinos involve individuals from their homeland who have also migrated to the United States. Imbued with sentiments of homeland camaraderie, recent-immigrant Latinos often affectionately refer to their friends as
paisanos or countrymen. *Paisanos* represent either pre-migration friendships
originating in their shared country of origin, or they are affiliations with countrymen that were established while in the U.S. Moreover, *paisanos* are people with whom some homeless Latinos deeply identify, given similarities in
their immigrant experiences. All-to-aware of the current anti-immigrant political climate in Los Angeles, Spanish speaking Latinos (both recent and
long-term residents) depend on the support of the few allies they have, their
paisanos. In Marcos' view (the recently immigrated man spoken of earlier)
the anti-immigrant political rhetoric has given many employers further justi-
fication for paying Latinos low and often exploitive wages. Marcos, like
many recent immigrant homeless men, maintains long-term relationships
with childhood friends (that originated in Mexico and continued while in the
U.S.)—who he relies on to lessen the many adversities he faces. *Paisano* relations are homeland bonds that continue to link these homeless Latinos
struggling to survive in the United States.

In contrast, the friendships of homeless, English speaking Latino (native-
born and long-term residents or more Americanized Latinos) display less social and emotional intimacy. Generally the English speaking ability of these
homeless Latinos enables them to better articulate their needs, facilitates their
integration within American society and lessens their occupational and economic exploitation, as compared to their Spanish speaking homeless peers.
Also, Americanized homeless Latinos are either native-born or legal, long-
term U.S. residents that primarily speak English and compared to recent immigrant Latinos they move freely through cities less fearful of authorities and
unconcerned about being deported. Consequently, they are less inclined to
share in this *paisano* sentiment and the enduring relationships that seem to be
a necessity for Spanish speaking Latinos (or recent-immigrants).

Although, both Americanized and recent-immigrant Latinos tend to have
small networks of friends, Americanized Latinos have known their friends
less time compared to recent-immigrant Latinos. Also, only a small percent
of Americanized Latinos report receiving emotional or moral support from
any of their affiliates, while twice as many of the recent-immigrant Latinos

have emotionally supportive friends and associates. And the friendships of Americanized Latinos manifest a primarily recreational nature. Meeting up with their friends around downtown L.A. generally involves just spending time talking, playing card games or, in some cases, entertaining themselves through alcohol or drug use. Drinking and doing drugs for recreational purposes among homeless men can include their entire network of friends, associates and acquaintances alike, yet conversations about the more personal aspects of their lives is usually reserved for close friends and sometimes close associates.

Basically, the relationships of Americanized Latino men fall into two categories: 1) friends they drink and hang out with and with which they exchange some resources; and 2) the few friends they can also intimately converse with about their problems and concerns. Even a homeless man like Ramon (an Americanized Latino), who has the good fortunate of having several individuals he can count on for help, only relies on one or two among them as confidants. Ramon has a network of three associates and two friends and although he has known some of his associates longer than some of his friends; his friends are individuals he shares his problems with, as well as, money and a few drinks. Furthermore, unlike recent-immigrant Latinos whose friendships consists of pre-migration relationships, with *paisanos*, or with other immigrants experiencing similar problems, most of the non-kin relationships of Americanized Latinos are with homeless men they meet up with on Skid Row. Only a few Americanized Latinos retain relationships established prior to their homelessness.

EXCHANGE CAPACITY:
THE DYNAMICS OF ASKING FRIENDS FOR HELP

Few homeless men are reserved about asking their friends for material or emotional support when needed. Friends are highly valued specifically because they can be counted on to provide some type of support. Typically, among all three groups of homeless men who solicit the help of friends do so with a regard for the following: 1) the urgency or immediacy of the need; 2) the particular individual to be asked and their circumstances; and 3) the specific kind of help that is needed. Maintaining amicable relations with friends, through a show of respect, understanding, trustworthiness and reciprocity, increases benevolence and comfort in engaging their support. Conversely, comfort enlisting the support of friends is negatively affected by breeches in friendship-role expectations, that is, by breeches in respect, trust and reciprocity.

Feeling comfortable asking friends for help makes getting help more likely; however, establishing such comfort involves interpersonal negotiations of normative behavior or role expectations within friendships. In Jack's situation (African American) his ease in turning to his friend Rafer lies in their mutual understanding that help is solicited only when truly needed:

> He's gonna give it if he figures I need it. That's the kind of relationship that we have . . . same is with him. Whatever the occasion might be, if I need it . . . if need be. I need some money . . . if he got it, I'll have it. If he don't have it he'll save money and I'm gonna have it. It's the same with me. Stuff I need, I need. If I don't need, I don't ask for what I don't need. He knows that, we have that type of rapport.

Being cognizant and considerate of possibly overburdening friends with incidental requests for help bolsters feelings of trust and respect in the relationships of people like Jack and Rafer. As they work to abide by their common role expectations in granting support for each other they also preserve the integrity of their friendship.

Recent-immigrant Latinos (primarily Spanish speakers) also resist becoming a burden to their friends. Most say their friends have and would assist them during hard times, but they feel ashamed of being homeless and of troubling their friends. Occasionally, they do ask friends for different types of help and very much appreciate receiving it, yet they shy away from asking too often. That these men are almost painfully hesitant to ask their friends for help might be attributed to: socialization and class processes that steer Latino men away from reliance on others for material help; or perhaps attributed to maintaining some semblance of individual self-sufficiency (or self-determination); and/or it may be a means of "salvaging the self" by averting the shame that often accompanies such requests (i.e., by not asking for help they maintain their personal dignity). Whichever interpretation is made of their wariness to ask for help, these men strive to earn a living by taking on even the most labor intensive jobs and at the lowest wages.

In the case of George (a Spanish speaking long-term resident who has been homeless for one month), he feels so ashamed of the situation he is in and of his personal appearance that he avoids the one friend that would readily help him, his friend Alfonso:[4]

> If I needed some emergency help . . . I would feel comfortable. I know that he would loan it to me if I asked him, talked to him. He would loan it to me, but I don't have the nerve to ask. That is, I don't dare ask him for a favor. But I know that he would do it for me if I asked him. He and I have helped each other much. He has asked me and I him. And we have never been asking for repayment . . .

it just ends there . . . at that. Also, it's not a lot of money that we ask each other for—from fifty down. Sometimes we've even gotten to one-hundred. But we've never paid each other back because we feel like brothers. Right now I haven't asked him for money because I don't feel . . . I feel ashamed. What's more I don't want to visit him . . . for him to see me like this, the way I am. Because he will scold me. He will tell me, "Why don't you call to the house?" "Why don't you come over?" And I lie to him . . . "No, it's that I'm in another area." But it's not that. I don't want him to see how I am. He's always seen me standing on top. He's never seen me on the street. I feel ashamed. [Trans.]

As the quote illustrates, George expresses confidence in his friend's willingness to help him, yet he stipulates that unless faced with an emergency (which in his opinion, his present state of homelessness is not), he will not ask him for help. Furthermore, he says that even in an emergency he would not ask without some reservation. By keeping his homeless predicament secret, George seems determined to preserve his self-image as a self-sufficient man. George values his friend's opinion of him and their continued friendship more than any resources he might gain in revealing the extent of his impoverishment. George's friendship reflects the experience of many of the participants in this study, as it is subjected to the effects of his change in status which produces inequities in the resource exchanges of once comparably situated friends. This, in turn, generates power differentials among friends that leave homeless individuals grappling with waves of emotions involving shame, guilt and sadness in the wake of a fall in social position. Nevertheless, both recent-immigrant Latinos and African Americans can indeed count on the help of close friends. For recent-immigrant Latinos, help comes mostly from housed friends, while among African Americans it is received from a mix of housed and homeless friends. However, both groups resist imposing on friends unless their need is truly urgent.

Americanized Latinos differ from recent-immigrants and from African Americans in this respect—their requests for help are less formal. Typically they do not even make requests for help as their relationships involve norms of mutually hanging out and helping out. For the most part, there seems to be no formal request for assistance among these men, they simply participate in a mutual sharing of resources throughout the course of their day. They have an unstated but observable comfort in just knowing that support (both emotional and material forms) is given as needed. Rafael (English speaking), a native-born Mexican American man, that has been homeless seven times in the last ten years, recounts the everyday exchange of resources that takes place between his friend Roberto and himself:

If I was a lucky one and I get a job, and he don't get a job . . . and he's on the streets and I got money and he don't got none . . . [motions with his hands giving money to another]. We been together so long. Sometimes he put money out of his pocket for myself. He will provide me a cigarette, a soda pop or meal. I think, yeah we provide each other . . . sometimes with money. Other than that, just friendship.

Like this Mexican American homeless man, many Americanized Latinos spoke of the daily sharing of resources with homeless friends.

Among Americanized and recent-immigrant Latino groups, differences in soliciting help from friends are in part due to the housing status of their friends. The majority of Americanized Latinos have friends that are also homeless; therefore, they are less fearful of being seen as undesirable by these individuals or of losing friendships because of their dubious homeless status. Basically, the friends of Americanized Latinos understand the ins and outs of homelessness because they share in the experience. Conversely, most recent-immigrant Latinos maintain friendships with employed, domiciled individuals who, though of low economic means, are able to maintain some economic self-sufficiency. Recent immigrant Latinos have a work ethos that reflects a desire to gain the kind of economic self-sufficiency that their steadily employed friends enjoy. Thus, not wanting to appear as failures in their attempts to provide for themselves, some recent-immigrant Latinos are saying little about or are completely hiding their homeless situation from friends.

In other instances, how apropos it is to make a request for help is linked to the personal circumstances of friends and this then becomes the defining principle. In Thomas' situation (an African American man), he offered support to his friend but hesitated to ask for any in return because Simon was grieving his mother's passing:

I wouldn't ask Simon for nothing, because he's like a brother to me . . . him and his mom . . . his mom passed away and I miss her so much. Her name is Thomas. Mrs. Thomas was like a mother to me. She was my usher-boy supervisor. And Simon and his brother, they're all like good people to me.

According to Thomas, the circumstances surrounding his friend's personal hardship (the death of someone they both cared for) presently defines the nature of their mutual networking. The successful ebb and flow of reciprocal activity in the networks of homeless friends, holds these compeers to careful considerations of opportune and inopportune moments for soliciting various kinds of support. Asking friends for help during obviously unfortunate times imparts sentiments of disrespect and lack of sympathy, which can ultimately weaken the foundation of these friendships. Knowing when to avoid asking for help is important for homeless men wishing to maintain a strong, supportive network of friends.

Furthermore, comfort in asking for support is affected by the solicitor's own personal circumstances, for example, a known drug addict cannot ask friends for money when he knows they are disturbed by his problem. Michael (African American) describes Kirk as a very good friend who will help him out with meals, sometimes with a place to sleep, let him watch television or even allow him access to his shower. However, because of Michael's drug problem, Kirk rarely gives him any money. Many times, Kirk has offered to help Michael get off drugs, but it is to no avail. Michael's history of drug abuse impedes his efforts to gain monetary aid from Kirk; although, other resources are provided. Assessments of personal circumstances, whether their own or those of others, enable homeless men to act appropriately within their networks and thus, keep supportive relationships intact.

Mindful of previous supportive exchanges, street men actively alternate their networking among many friends depending on the desired resource. For some homeless African American men, knowing that friends can be counted on for help matters more than the frequency with which they actually exchange resources. One man, Jerry (African American), pointed out the taken for granted nature of counting on friends, stating that the real issue is who to turn to for a specific kind of assistance:

> I would be comfortable with any of them, asking for help . . . but who would be able to provide that assistance at the time needed would be probably a more correct question. Like certain things that I might need . . . like say I feel like smoking a joint, I'm not going to say, "Hey Ted, I need to smoke a joint."

In the quote above, Jerry speaks of the impropriety of asking his friend Ted, the shelter director for a marijuana cigarette even though Jerry says he uses this drug for medicinal purposes. Clearly, comfort in asking friends for help is also contingent on the kind of help that is required and who is available to provide it. Having larger friendship networks becomes a major plus in securing various resources, including drugs. Perhaps many homeless men use illegal drugs primarily to get high and pass the time; however, for Jerry smoking marijuana alleviates his cancer symptoms. Unlike many cancer patients who are prescribed marijuana cigarettes to help ease their pain, up to this point Jerry had not received a prescription and is forced to obtain these cigarettes through illegal means. For the most part, homeless African American men maintain relationships with friends that enable them to feel comfortable soliciting their support. Being comfortable relying on friends for help is linked to overall feelings of respect, understanding, compassion and affection among network members.

Power Differentials and Role Identification: Along Gender Lines

Additionally, friendships are sustained by individual efforts to first consider the personal circumstances of their friends prior to requesting their assistance. For instance, given the harshness of homeless life, homeless men tend to empathize with their female counterparts, they: are concerned about their survival; try to protect them; and avoid asking for their help. To be sure, homeless Latino and African American men do sometimes turn to female friends for material assistance, yet they seem especially cautious in doing so. It should be noted, however, that funding constraints limited the scope of this study to an examination of the lives of minority, homeless men and required the exclusion of homeless women. Hence, the accounts presented are from the perspective of homeless men and no attempts were made to seek out the women (both homeless and housed) that could corroborate their stories.

However, limited non-participant observation of homeless women suggests that they require the protection and material support of the homeless men they associate with. If street life is tough on men it is doubly tough on women, who are apt to be more vulnerable to threats of violence. Thus, homeless women seek out the companionship of men for personal protection and material help, such as: money; a motel room to spend the night; and sometimes recreational drugs. According to James, an African American man:

> Annie, this is the girl that just passed here. She lived with me at the Frontier Motel for a while, when ever I'm there. For downtown, she's a good woman. She looks out for me as well. She's been down here longer than I have so she tells me who to be involved with and who to leave alone. And I'm forty-two years old and of course I know these things, but she reassures that for me. She won't let anyone take advantage of me while we're together. Even though like I'll spend my unemployment checks with her a lot of the time. I been used in that respect, so that's a facade, a front that she puts up that she's looking out for me. I just ride along with it and stuff. I enjoy her company. Someone to talk to and if I want some sexual satisfaction she's there . . . As a matter of fact, through doing drugs I guess she feels that's a pay back. Sometimes I don't even care for them, but you know she sort of insists so I just cater to her with that.

As indicated above, women downtown often seek monetary support, recreational drugs and companionship, while, men look to women for emotional support and sexual relations. Homeless men and women retain gender roles that guide their behavior where material exchanges are concerned. In this kind of supportive posturing, homeless men identify themselves, and are identified by female counterparts, as "protectors" and/or "providers" of financial or material resources. Conversely, women become identified as emotional and physical intimates. By reinforcing each other's roles they subsequently, strengthen the asymmetrical power differentials present in their relationships. That is, the dependence of homeless women on the kindness of homeless men is intensified by such role ascriptions.

The vignettes to follow indicate that Latinos and African American homeless men alike express some discomfort in asking either homeless or housed women for help. Ray (African American man) expressed concern about his friend Beverly, who sleeps in a box across the street from his own make-shift tent:

> Beverly is a friend of mine who lives on the street corner, in a box. Right across the street from where you saw me. I've known her for about twelve years. She something like a sister to me. She had the misfortune of getting busted; going to jail . . . came back and had nothing. And had to move into a box and so she's not doing so well now. But we still stay in contact. Before she went to jail, she was doing real well financially and so forth. She has provided for me in the past, but she's not in any position to provide me with any help now. I try to provide help for her, when I come up with any extra money or something . . . I kind of contribute to her cause.

In part, homeless men hesitate to ask women for help because this runs counter to their socially prescribed roles as men, which dictate that they act as providers and protectors. The African American men interviewed actually tend to provide more tangible aid for their female friends than they gain in return.

Also echoing a masculine protective sentiment toward women, Art (an African American man) freely turns to his male friends for monetary loans and other resources, but is adamantly opposed to asking his girlfriend for assistance:

> I don't like asking her for help. I don't like to. I don't feel very comfortable. I don't feel comfortable asking a lady for anything . . . I don't!

Art's girlfriend Sandy does provide him with emotional support, sexual relations and shares most of her resources with him, however, Art seldom directly asks her for help. Although, there is an understanding among street friends that they can count on each other to give what they can, socially learned gender roles keep homeless men from feeling comfortable requesting monetary help from the women they know. Art does most of the financial providing in his relationship with Sandy, still he sees her as an equal contributor:

> It's fair exchange on our part, we give to each other to help each other out. I do anything for her, I think she do anything for me.

Friends are an important avenue of support for African American men, most of which feel comfortable turning to friends of either gender for help. These men express a good deal of certainty that their friends would provide any assistance within their means. Many of these men simply preferred not to ask homeless women for financial assistance.

In the case of Americanized Latinos, their friendships are mostly with housed women who, because of their more advantageous economic position, can and do provide them with financial support. Only a small percent of Americanized Latinos interviewed spoke of having friendships with women. Americanized Latinos had established such ties prior to becoming homeless. Overall, Latinos in both groups maintain platonic relations with the women they befriend, in contrast to African American men who tended to have physically intimate relationships with female friends.

Julian, a young twenty-four year old Latino man (Americanized, English speaking, long-term resident originally from Nicaragua) relies on the mothering nature of a woman named Elva. In describing Elva, Julian says,

> She's an old lady. She's got two daughters. One is almost my age and the other one is ten I think. But she only lives with the little one. When I met her we became very close because she told me a story that she had a baby and the baby died . . . and if he was alive right now he would be my age. Emotionally she's always there for me. She gives me advice. I can depend on her.

Julian further explains that he does not want to burden Elva, thus, he fails to take advantage of this Christian women's continuous offers to help.

Jose is an immigrant from Mexico who having lived in the United States for more than ten years (a Spanish-speaking, long-term resident), has the misfortune of being chronically homeless throughout a good deal of this time. The last time Jose had a place to stay he was living in Yuma, Arizona with his friend Juan who recently passed away. During that time Jose worked full-time harvesting crops in the orange fields. Soon after the death of his friend, Jose made his way to Los Angeles where he became acquainted with three women, Rosamaria, Camelia and Nicco—all of whom (as Jose insinuated) are illegal immigrants that ironically sleep under the stairs of the Immigration and Naturalization building.

Come night fall, Rosamaria, Camelia and Nicco return to their sleeping area. At this point they pick-up their blankets and sleeping bags from Jose, who stores them during the day at the home of a nearby acquaintance. Reminiscent of housewives providing meals for their families, almost without failing, soon after arriving at their resting area the women begin sharing food and beer with Jose and his friend. Jose has not actually asked them for any kind of help, they simply take it upon themselves to share whatever they have with him. Given their consistent generosity, Jose is sure they would gladly oblige him if he requested their help. As Jose says,[5]

> I consider them my friends because they sometimes come at night with food. And like I told you, sometimes they bring beer . . . they buy me a beer. Not because of a vice that I have to be drinking beer, but because they come and . . . They say to me, "Jose would you like a beer or something to eat?" That's why I consider them my friends. Right now they will arrive there, where my things are. I don't know what they are doing. If they are working or I don't know what they are doing. Everyday they have money . . . I don't know what they are into. They may be in prostitution or . . . I'm not interested in that. They don't bother me. They share with me and I also; when I have money because I have worked . . . I share with them. If they ask me, "Lend me five, lend me six dollars." [Trans.]

Overall, Jose is comfortable accepting the help offered by Rosamaria, Camelia and Nicco, so much so that he refrains from making a personal judgment about their possible "call-girl" activities.

Over the long run, navigating through the hazards of life on the streets leads a small number of homeless Latino men and homeless women into supportive exchanges that assume modes of behavior somewhat similar to those witnessed among African Americans. Regarding their relations with homeless women there are, however, two observable differences among these Latino long-term or chronically homeless street dwellers and African American men that are similarly situated: 1) Latino participants maintain platonic relationships with their female "street" friends; and 2) homeless women do most of the providing—giving food, beer and even pocket change to these men. In return Latino men offer them a few material resources (usually in the form of small monetary loans) and primarily, protection by ensuring their personal safety while they sleep outdoors.

All homeless men interviewed preserved their friendships and thus, their networks by adhering to role expectations (both as friends and in terms of gender ascriptions) and through their awareness and concern about the personal circumstances of other network members. Within friendship networks, requests for help were varied among members. Decisions regarding who to ask for help take into account: 1) who can provide the required resource; and 2) whether it is appropriate to ask this member. Comfort procuring the support of friendship networks then, takes on either a role-related mode (wherein, friendship roles, gender roles and shared normative prescriptions are considered) or a more pragmatic mode (wherein, the specific need itself determines who will be approached for assistance).

RECIPROCITY: THE HALLMARK OF FRIENDSHIPS

Perceptions of reciprocity in resource exchange also influence the freedom
with which homeless compeers solicit each other's help. An appreciable level
of reciprocity of both tangible (sustenance) and subjective (emotional support) resources encourages positive personal linkages that in turn promote ongoing exchanges among friends. Reciprocity, whether emotionally or materially based, is a fundamental component in all relationships—particularly
among friends. Where reciprocity is consistently lacking, a break in relationships may be inevitable even among close friends. For homeless men reciprocity, like friendship itself, is linked to overall feelings of trust, respect and
assurances of genuine affection or concern. Reciprocity may well be the hallmark of many Skid Row relationships, yet the manner in which favors are re-
turned varies depending on the individual and his or her resources. It seems
that among homeless men reciprocating in kind is not as significant in sus-
taining amicable relationships, as is the demonstration of a reciprocal de-
pendability. Reciprocity is linked to the activation of social capital through
the perceived willingness to repay mutually accumulated social debts (Lin
2001). Knowing that friends can be counted on to lend a hand when needed,
goes a long way in strengthening the social linkages of African American
street men like, Mark:

> Me and Louis, we go way back to a . . . downtown. I met him about fourteen
> years ago. We're close. We're always talking about things like what's really go-
> ing on around us . . . people and attitudes and stuff. To me Louis is my best
> friend. I can rely on Louis to do something for me when I need something. Say
> I need a little change . . . ten dollars; Louis will give it to me without even ask-
> ing me what I need it for. And that's a friend see. If you loan somebody some-
> thing you don't ask them, "What do you want it for?" As long as you know he's
> going to give it back to you and that's the way it's suppose to be.

In turn, Mark helps Louis out by doing whatever his friend might need, like
cleaning his room at the shelter where they both stay when Louis is busy with
other shelter duties to take care of it himself. Mark says that depending on
what comes up; Louis is probably the first person he turns to for help. Reciprocity is so well established for Mark and Louis that their relationship is distinguished by a mutual trust in one another's intentions and reliability.

The intent to reciprocate, even if unable to actually do so is an acceptable and understandable occurrence among homeless friends. However,
simply ignoring the implied principle of reciprocity in friendships sets dis-
ruptive practices in motion that unravel even close ties. Among participants in this study, African American men were most vocally intolerant of

breeches in the norm of reciprocity. Although, as Jerry (African American) points out, sometimes friends may want to help but find themselves incapable of rendering assistance:

> There's always a reason, it might be short of funds . . . might be the time, might be something that cannot be done anytime soon. So there's always a reason.

Usually patterns of reciprocity are long established and the intentions of friends are well known. Should it become evident that a friend is deliberately taking but not giving resentments begin and friendship are threatened. Generally speaking, homeless African American and Latino men seldom tolerate being hustled by people they thought were their friends and few second chances are given to people that take unfair advantage of them. In speaking of his friend Charles, another African American man, James, expresses his frustration:

> Charles gets around a lot . . . [Edited] I don't know if he's visiting family or what, but he's a fuck-up too! Excuse my language; he's a screw ball too. I don't expect to see him, he owes me money also.

Strong resentments form when friends are delinquent in paying back loans, because homeless lenders themselves have such scarce capital. Among many homeless men (particularly among African American and Americanized Latinos) money is exchanged with the understanding that even small amounts must be paid back, and the word spreads quickly when someone violates this implicit loan agreement. As illustrated above, unless Charles repays the money he borrowed from James, he will probably be cut off from future loans within this circle of Skid Row friends.

Conclusion

This chapter has explored the saliency that friendship bonds have in the lives of homeless Latino and African American men. How these men initiate and maintain friendships with both housed and homeless individuals was also examined. And in line with the findings of notable researchers (Cohen and Sokolovsky 1989; LaGory, et. al. 1991; Snow and Anderson 1993) this study confirms that, in their repertoire of relations, many homeless men do have close attachments and interactions with significant others. Further, we have seen that such ties can be both instrumentally and emotionally valuable. And while researchers caution that, " . . . such support is essentially accommodative rather than curative," (Snow and Anderson 1993:196) the survival value of close affiliations should not be underestimated. Indeed homeless friendships serve an instrumental function, as Ray (an African American man) indicates surviving street life hinges on the mutual support of friends. However, as he points out below the bottom line (literally) is that the level of social intimacy among them is crucial to their survival:

> This is what I call my pivot point. These are the people I know regardless of who else ever I meet. Whatever it carries me into . . . but these are the people that are concerned about where I've been and where I'm going and headed. We're concerned like that about each other . . . [Edited] I feel like its ok because my friendships are ones of necessity usually. These are friendships that we have with each other that have to be! Not that just are. I mean we all perform some function with each other . . . and see eye to eye for most. And that's what our survival is based on—whether we care about each other.

In this landscape of cardboard houses and seemingly endless nights, friends perform two, among other, important functions: first, they facilitate survival by providing companionship or a partnership, if you will, for negotiating the environment; and the second concerns their compensatory function which is most purposeful among socially intimate individuals.

Recognizing that homeless men engage in various types of social relations (e.g., from casual acquaintances, to associates, to friendships) enhances our understanding of the active and rational capacity of many homeless people. In turn, by virtue of this perceptual shift (i.e., crediting these men with negotiating their survival versus labeling them socially pathological and disaffiliated) they become a population that while facing many problems, can be transitioned into conventional housing. In other words, a clear view of the troubles and the resources of this extremely impoverished population is needed in order to avoid being overwhelmed by this crisis of homelessness in America.

NOTES

1. Spanish quote:"Pues lo considero porque el me a brindado muchas de las veces . . . me a brindado su casa, como el es casado. A veces que me mira asi que no trabajo, muchas de las veces me a ofrecido dinero. Y pues el me a dicho que cuando necesite un favor o algo que acuda a el. Por eso lo considero mi amigo."

2. Spanish quote:"Porque pues es el unico amigo que tengo todo mi vida. Porque el desde diesiocho años andamos juntos. Anduvimos juntos pues . . . Nos venimos a este país y pues el se caso aqui. Tiene su hogar y todo. Y siempre que yo necesito algo yo voy con el. Pero ultimamente no voy con el porque su señora es muy . . . no se no me puede ver la señora de el."

3. Spanish quote:"No paso asi imprevistamente. A pesar de que nos venimos con tiempo diferentes. Pero nos venimos encontrando un día los tres por casualidad en la Broadway. Y pues me han sabido dar la mano hasta hoy . . . [*edited*] Nos la llevamos bien. Tratamos de sobrellevar todos los problemas que hay entre nosotros. Comunicarnos que es lo que esta pasando y asi . . . pues a veces ellos me dicen de algun empleo y voy a verificar a ver si todavia ocupan aquella persona o no. Nos vamos a los parques a pasar un tiempo libre, como los Domingos. Y asi sucesivamente cada fin de semana."

4. Spanish quote:"Si yo necesitara una ayuda de urgencia, me sentiria cómodo . . . yo se que si me la présta diciendole, hablandole. Me lo présta . . . pero no me ánimo a decirle. O sea, que no me atrevo a pedirle un favor. Pero yo se que si me lo hace si yo se lo pido. Yo y el nos hemos ayudado mucho. El me a pedido a mi y yo a el. Y nunca nos hemos andado cobrando . . . hay queda. Tambien no es mucho dinero que nos pedimos, de cincuenta para bajo. A veces hasta sien ya hemos llegado. Pero nunca nos hemos pagado . . . porque nos sentimos como hermanos. Orita no le e pedido dinero porque, no me siento . . . me siento con vergüenza que yo . . . es mas no quiero visitarlo que me vea asi como ando. Porque me va regañar, me va decir, "¿Porque no me hablas a la casa?" "¿Porque no vienes?" Y le hecho mentiras, "No, es que estoy en otra parte." Pero no es eso, no quiero que me mire como ando. A mi siempre me ha mirado el parado, arriba. Nunca me ha mirado en la calle. Me da vergüenza."

5. Spanish quote:"A ellas las considero mis amigas porque tambien ellas en veces vienen con comida en las noches. Y como digo, en veces train cerveza . . . me compran una cerveza. No por el vicio que tenga yo de estar tomando cerveza, si no que ellas llegan y . . . ellas me dicen, "¿Jose quieres una cerveza o quieres comer algo?" Por eso las considero mis amigas . . . orita ellas llegan allí donde estan mis cosas. No se que andaran haciendo. Si andaran trabajando o no se que andan haciendo. Ellas todos los días train dinero, yo no se que harán. Andaran en la prostitucíon o . . . no me interesa eso. Ellas no se meten con migo. Ellas comparten con migo y yo tambien quando traigo dinero que trabajo, yo comparto con ellas . . . si me piden, "Préstame cinco, préstame sies dolares.""

Chapter Six

A Valuable Component
in the Larger Mosaic of Solutions

The central organizing themes explored throughout this work include the autonomy and centrality of individual action as the source of social meaning (i.e., human agency); this in turn was integrally linked to the assumption that homeless individuals are rational decision makers that can and do negotiate their social worlds;[1] and further, I emphasized that all such action is carried out within the limits of impeding structural forces (e.g., extreme poverty, excessive unemployment, lack of affordable housing, and the harsh social context of Skid Row). Social networks and the interpersonal investments of their members then are the rational outcome of the survival strategies exercised by homeless men. Survival strategies that not only facilitate the acquisition of much needed resources, but also improve the overall quality of their lives out on the streets. Social support researchers have documented the positive impact that even a perception of social support has on an individual's psychological well-being (Sarason, et. al. 1994; Cohen and McKay 1984). The significance of social support networks among homeless people must be understood because institutional solutions tend toward removing homeless persons from meaningful sources of support (Ennett, et. al. 1999), because many of these agencies view homeless relationships as deviant. To increase their effectiveness, policy initiatives and intervention programs should maximize the sources of social support already available to homeless individuals, as these may provide essential coping mechanisms. Consequently, the social or personal networks of homeless men are a small yet valuable component in the larger mosaic of solutions to American homelessness that all policy minded researchers ought to consider.

SUMMARY OF FINDINGS

Chapter one provided a statement of the problem under study, namely, the importance of examining the role social networks play in the daily survival of homeless men. Here, I articulated the need for conducting a comparative, in-depth analysis of the homeless experiences of African Americans and two groups of Latinos (Americanized Latinos who are either native-born or long-term U.S. residents and recent-immigrant Latinos who are Spanish speakers and are usually identified as day laborers and/or undocumented workers). Table 1.0 presents the demographic characteristics of 21 Latino and 20 African American homeless participants in this study. Further, in this chapter I discussed a number of theoretical perspectives on homeless men, beginning with views that tend to blame homeless victims for their troubles by espousing some type of "personality deficit" explanation of their situation (disaffiliation theorists), and following with views that overly victimize homeless people by overemphasizing the impact of structural forces on their lives (dislocation theorists). I end by offering a social networking perspective on the situation homelessness that recognizes the extent to which homeless men act on their own behalf. Linked to earlier discussions of human agency, this perspective takes an empowering view of homeless men that are engaged in struggles to survive — with a little help from their friends (as well as, from acquaintances and a few associates). In the second chapter I set out to respond to the following research questions:

1) How do informal social networks operate for homeless Latino as compared to homeless African American men?
2) How are social networks initiated, maintained or weakened?
3) How do the social networks of recent Latino immigrants (or Spanish speakers) compare to those of long-term residents and/or native-born Latinos (or English speakers)?

Chapter three provides a detailed examination of the informal non-kin networks that exists among homeless Latinos and African Americas and includes descriptions of the forms and functioning of their respective networks. The use of a literal definition of homelessness is also discussed and data on the emergent structural properties of social networks was analyzed and presented in tabled form (tables 3.1 and 3.2). Some of the key findings presented in chapter three are as follows: 1) networking is greatest among African Americans and Americanized Latinos, compared to recent-immigrant Latinos, as indicated by the larger size of their networks; 2) compared to recent-immigrant Latinos, African American and Americanized Latinos interacted more frequently with network members; 3) recent-immigrant Latinos, however, report having closer relationships with their network members than did Americanized Latinos and African Americans; 4) all three groups report a high level of reciprocity in resource exchange; and 5) the flow and types of resources varied among the three groups.

The saliency of weak ties in the everyday lives of homeless men, chapter four, is revealed through detailed descriptions of their casual relationships with acquaintances and associates. Here, I found that homeless men ranked their affiliates based on perceived levels of social intimacy, trust and a willingness to provide support. According to their hierarchy of affiliations, casual acquaintances are numerously held ties that carry few mutual expectations, and act as a kind of satellite link in receiving and transmitting information throughout Skid Row. The associates of homeless men emerge, based on descriptions provided in chapter three, as more instrumentally oriented or utilitarian linkages. These relations are imbued with moderate levels of social intimacy, and are primarily motivated by their capacity for resource exchange. The significance of this chapter lies in its affirmation of the hierarchy of affiliations existing among homeless men and the meaningful role played by even their tenuous ties.

Next, chapter five, examines the socially intimate bonds maintained by homeless men—their friendships. In response to the notion that all linkages existing among homeless men are necessarily (given their supposed transient nature), tenuous and shallow, I asked whether homeless men had friends they could count on for help. They responded affirmatively and with definite ideas in mind about who ranked as a friend—and who did not. Unlike their more casual affiliations, friends were regarded as socially intimate, with affection and trust, and were usually known for a lengthy period of time. The chapter further explored the factors impacting friendship among homeless men (table 5.1). While these ties are instrumental in offering tangible support (albeit, infrequent), as indicated by the description offered above they are notably expressive linkages. Overall, the findings suggest that the networks of Americanized Latinos and African Americans facilitate their integration into a subculture of street life. While, those of recent-immigrant Latinos revolve around their immigrant struggles to find work, avoid deportation, and rely on the support of *paisanos* (countrymen).

POLICY IMPLICATION AND FUTURE RESEARCH

Taking a social networking approach to the study of minority homelessness in America's inner-cities, provides a keen basis for analyzing how hard pressed individuals mediate the structures of poverty that surround them. And while much has been said about the limited value of the social networks of the poor (e.g., the networks of poor minority group members are characterized as small, kin-based and dense, compared to the wide ranging, diverse networks of whites; Snow and Anderson 1993; Griffith 1985; Mindel 1980), nevertheless, among homeless men they are a mitigating factor improving the quality of their lives. Yes, the social networks of homeless men can offer only modest resources and they are "essentially accommodative rather than curative" (Snow and Anderson, 1993:196), yet at their core they represent the organized effort of poor people to change their circumstances.

This study supports Wagner's (1993) findings that, given the difficulty of their situation, many homeless individuals develop a communal sense of solidarity and relied on extensive social and/or personal networks of casual affiliates and friends (Wagner 1993). Wagner reminds us that the "researcher's approach is always influenced by ideology and personal characteristics as framing forces in what he or she will find," (1993:40) within the scope of my research this should be taken to mean that I (like Wagner), challenge the belief that homeless people are completely disempowered.

A major ramification of viewing homeless individuals as overly-victimized or made helpless by the nature of their extreme impoverishment is that, as we see them so shall we advocate for them. In other words, helpless people must by definition become dependent on the services generated to ameliorate their situation. The politics of compassion, as Hoch (1989) have noted, has erroneously led to policies of shelterization and segregation of homeless people. Advocates for homeless individuals pushing for their "right to shelter" have managed to institute policies that seek to treat their maladies and contain them in designated areas (Hoch 1989). Shelters, as 'total institutions' (Stark 1994), exercise complete control over their clients and create dependence, and containment policies are just short of re-instituting segregation (Hoch 1989).

If providing emergency shelter is not the solution to homelessness, what is? First of all, we must understand the dimensions of the problem of homelessness—both micro and macro. That is, we need a holistic approach that seeks a deeper understanding of the diversity of the population and their fundamentally different experiences of homelessness, at the micro level—as well as, an understanding of the larger socioeconomic structures that have contributed to homelessness, at the macro level.

Moreover, the impact of macro level forces (i.e., economic restructuring, globalization, unemployment, rising poverty, shortage of low-income housing and reductions in welfare benefits) on individuals is seldom taken as a primary explanation for the troubles encountered by those with limited economic resources, particularly because not all individuals are affected in the same way. Common sense notions or folk understandings tend to rely on explanations that provide simplified reasons for individual troubles, such as individual pathologies or deficits. The fact that social structural conditions put people at risk for extreme poverty and thus, for homelessness is often nullified by quick and clouded explanations that center on individuals. This focus on simple reasons for complex problems undermines the development of effective policy measures.

Any serious attempt to redress the increasing social and economic inequity must start with macro-scale forces (equitable distribution of the nation's wealth and resources). Unfortunately, policy measures usually take an ameliorative approach to poverty and homelessness, which means both are likely to grow (e.g., most attention and funding given to emergency services and seldom to the development of preventive programs). Minimally, the large scale policy changes needed to end homelessness in the U.S. would require: 1) increase in the minimum wage (livable wages); 2) increase in low and semi-skilled job opportunities as legitimate employment opportunities are associated with diminishing episodes of homelessness (Wong and Piliavin 1997); 3) expanding earned income-tax credits for low-income people (and families); 4) welfare programs geared toward moving people out of poverty; 5) significantly increasing government housing subsidies and the stocks of affordable housing to reduce the need for emergency shelter services—as researchers indicate that stable, affordable housing facilitates the transition from a street to mainstream lifestyle (Weitzman et al. 1990); and 6) major expansion of job training and placement programs. While emergency services such as meal and shelter facilities are very much needed, the policy aim should be to quickly transition individuals into more permanent housing arrangements.

From a network analytic approach, homelessness researchers and policy makers must consider the value implicit (if not explicit) in the network affiliations cultivated by homeless individuals that enable their daily survival on the streets of Skid Row. As sources of social support, such relationships accomplish what even the most well meaning and dedicated service providers cannot—they provide homeless men with a measure of self-sufficiency, self-esteem and have the capacity to foster social, emotional well-being (Toohey, et. al. 2004). Mindful of the damaging effects of becoming acculturated into a Skid Row way of life (i.e., succumbing to the pathologies of life on the streets), service providers often discourage and restrict their homeless clients from maintaining "outside contacts" or personal relationships when participating in their programs (Bogard, et. al. 1999). In light of the present study's findings, this practice can be problematic because network participation enables many homeless men to continue to build and activate the social capital needed to obtain important (albeit meager) resources, and most importantly to do so willingly and as active agents in negotiating their own survival. Imbued within some of their network relationships is the power to provide more than ameliorating resources, such ties can also influence behavior in positive and protective ways (Toohey, et. al. 2004). African American and Latino individuals have long relied upon the social capital embedded within their non-kin ties as a means of negotiating the strains of poverty (e.g., these provide resources that delay and/or offset over-reliance on shelters and other public service programs; see Hopper and Milburn 1996). Thus, the relational attributes (relationships) present within the personal networks of homeless men can be instrumental in contributing to their overall well-being; what's more some of these networks are potentially equipped to facilitate their transition back into permanent housing (Toohey, et. al. 2004; Bao, et. al. 2000). In fact this study affirms Mercier and Racine's (1993) findings relating to the importance of social support. These researchers found that homeless-street people with access to even one consistently supportive acquaintance or friend were more successful in transitioning from a "street" to a "more mainstream" lifestyle (Mercier and Racine 1993). Through their participation in personal networks homeless men in this study actively work to negotiate homelessness and ensure their own survival by maintaining access to supportive, albeit humble, ties.

Future Directions

The lessons taken from the efforts of homeless men to access social or personal networks and thus, to activate social capital as a means of providing for their overall wellbeing are threefold: 1) to recognize the active agency of homeless men in negotiating the structures of poverty that surround them (as they actively initiate, participate in, and maintain personal networks); 2) to understand the continued importance of providing various forms of social support when needed without continuing to stigmatize already hard-pressed individuals for their situation of poverty (i.e., individual deficit models that tend to blame the victim); and 3) to acknowledge the need to adopt a multileveled perspective on the nature and causes of homelessness (i.e., maintaining a comprehensive and acute understanding of the complex social forces that contribute to homelessness involving both micro and macro factors). On this last point, it's important to identify the fundamental structural arrangements and patterns in society and the individual biographic factors that converge to generate and aggravate the state of homelessness in America.

A national policy is needed that deals with the lack of affordable housing and the increasingly entrenched nature of poverty found in urban ghettos. Ultimately, policy changes ought to involve structures that feed into our domestic economy, such as: the educational system that must respond to the needs of a more globally oriented market place by preparing underprivileged individuals for new job opportunities; the inner-cities must be economically revitalized in order to improve the quality of life for residents and for the generations to come; and also national changes in housing policy that provide short-term assistance (for instance, providing housing subsidies for low-income single men and women, as is presently provided for woman with children, that do not force their containment in Skid Row) and longer-term remedies involving the development of affordable housing that encourages home-ownership rather than the development of more government housing projects (which are also containment oriented).

A national policy must be broad enough to effect large scale changes, and tailored enough to address the specific problems encountered by various homeless groups (whether they are Latino, African American, white or other). Consequently, in order to successfully implement corrective policy measures we must call on researchers to continue their efforts to deepen our understanding (through both qualitative and quantitative methods) of the diversity of homelessness experiences nationwide. This is important because policies implemented to help one group may not work for another and we must assist, not hamper, homeless people in their struggles to exit the constraints of poverty and homelessness. There is an urgent need to understand that the ramifications of rising poverty rates, economic polarization, and blocked economic opportunities are visible in the growing rate of homelessness. Also, that without the political will to significantly increase the social and economic prospects of at risk populations, homelessness will remain a permanent and growing feature of American life despite the efforts of impoverished people to negotiate their survival by enlisting the social support of their acquaintances, associates and/or friends.

This work has sought to illuminate the many significant and meaningful ways in which homeless men act, against the odds, to ensure their own survival given the prospect of facing many more endless nights without a home. Through their active participation in and their ongoing attempts to maintain social networks, homeless men in this study were able to negotiate their situations of homelessness by activating the social capital necessary to facilitate a steady flow of needed resources. By engaging the support mechanisms present within their networks, that yield at best humble resources, many of these men acted daily to make their situation one that was indeed, *Homeless Not Hopeless*.

NOTE

1. I speak here of homeless men who are not suffering from a disorienting mental illness. There is of course, a segment of the population of homeless individuals that are made less competent by mental illness or also by excessive substance abuse (e.g., frequent crack users, heroin users, and alcoholics).

Appendix

Methods and Procedures

This study primarily analyzes data acquired through a series of qualitative in-depth interviews and non-participant observations that were conducted with a homeless case sample of 21 Latino and 20 African American participants. Through this qualitative methodological approach I provide a detailed account of the subjective experiences of the homeless individuals participating in this study. The in-depth qualitative interview method is commonly used to generate first person accounts of particular life experiences of people under study, which enables further exploration of emerging substantive themes. However, in-depth interviews soliciting extended personal accounts of specific life experiences can be very time consuming; therefore, to in order to expedite the process of data collection participants were also asked to respond to a brief background information survey. The survey data generated serves to supplement the qualitative data collected, by supplying information on the participant's history of homelessness, their marital status, residential history, employment history, and level of educational training.

With the help of an interview staff, homeless men in Los Angeles and East Los Angeles were interviewed from 1996 to 1998. My interview staff consisted of bilingual Latinos (fluent in Spanish and English), African American and white interviewers that had prior experiences working with homeless individuals in Los Angeles. Fortunately, I was able to recruit interviewers that were thoroughly trained to conduct ethnographic and survey interviews from a large California based research organization in which we were all previously employed a year prior to the onset of my study. Furthermore, several pilot interviews were conducted in order to test the preliminary survey and qualitative instruments. Soon after reviewing the pilot instruments, interviewing of homeless individuals began.

Furthermore, I acquired extensive field experience, first through my work as a research consultant for the RAND Corporation (a nonprofit research organization in Santa Monica, California) and secondly, while undertaking research activities for this study. I conducted field observations of homeless Latinos and African Americans in the Skid Row and west-side areas of Los Angeles. Moreover, while working on the "Course of Homelessness Study" for the RAND Corporation, I spent over a year and a half interviewing, maintaining contact with and getting to know homeless individuals. Through this experience I became aware of ethnic group differences in the daily survival strategies of homeless minority-group members. That is, reliance on certain institutional services (whether bed or meal facilities), interpersonal contact and assistance appeared to vary among Latinos and African Americans.

Based on my casual observations I decided to conduct an empirical investigation of the ethnic differences in the experience of homelessness. Consequently, I spent another year among homeless people and service providers in Skid Row and East Los Angeles—conducting qualitative interviews and nonparticipant observations.

DETERMINING WHO IS HOMELESS

In order to determine who is homeless I employ a definition of literal homelessness, that is, individuals are literally homeless if they have spent even one night of the last 30 nights sleeping in: 1) a shelter or mission; 2) public outdoor places (streets, parks, beaches and under freeway overpasses); and 3) in abandoned buildings or in cars and other vehicles. A randomly selected sample of approximately 41 Latino and African American participants was drawn from homeless shelters, meal facilities and the streets of the Los Angeles (Skid Row) and the East Los Angeles area (Rossi 1989).

QUALITATIVE RESEARCH

Because this study examines how social network processes operate for homeless African Americans and Latinos, the analysis essentially requires a focus on the insider's experience. Qualitative research methods generate detailed, rich descriptions of the social processes people engage in, thus, preserving the complexities of everyday life while facilitating a comprehensive analysis (Geertz 1983; Katz 1983). This methodology seems best suited for the type of process oriented analysis of social networks I am interested in conducting. A highly structured quantitative research design would preclude a deeper, holistic understanding of how people go about maintaining and/or weakening their network ties.

Key criticisms often levied against qualitative research methodologies, whether involving ethnographic fieldwork or in-depth interview techniques, often note a lack of tests for assessing the validity and reliability of the data generated (Katz 1983). Yet the supposition that qualitative research and analysis should conform to the credibility procedures set for quantitative analysis, contradicts the intrinsically emic orientation of this approach. On the issue of the lack of reliability measures in qualitative analysis as compared to those available in quantitative methods, Katz (1983:140) writes:

> If rules for coding are specified before data are gathered, the researcher can produce specialized, statistical evidence on the extent of agreement among "judges" who independently apply the scheme to the same data. This strategy is inconsistent with qualitative research. By definition, so long as a researcher's encounters with data are governed by preset coding rules, they cannot be exploited to develop qualifications in substantive analytic categories.

The conclusions reached through descriptive studies are not merely conjecture or impressionistic. The evaluation of the accuracy of qualitative data interpretation takes on what Katz (1983:147) refers to as an 'evidentiary' character for the reader and researcher, wherein, "the analytic method confers on readers unique powers to make their own judgments on reliability from independent encounters with data." Basically, readers themselves can scrutinize the qualitative researcher's consistency in interpreting the data, and the validity of their emerging concepts to the expressed experiences of participants (Katz 1983). This kind of evaluation provides an all-in-one credibility check that I find substantive and rigorous.

In-depth Interview Topics

The in-depth qualitative interviews conducted cover topics relating to the formation, maintenance and weakening of social networks. In-depth interviews start by asking participants to describe an ordinary day in their lives, and continue with open-ended questions that follow five topics of inquiry: 1) encounters with social service agencies; 2) their social relations; 3) their labor market experiences; and 4) their migration related experiences. The "ordinary day" question helps to initiate a more naturalistic process of inquiry that then leads into questions on specific topics involving social networks. There is some variation in the topics that individuals were be asked to discuss, depending on the relevancy of the topic to particular ethnic group members. For all participants in the study, the in-depth interviews focused on: the social networking context of their current episode of homelessness and inquires about aspects of their pre-homeless life experiences. The topics we discussed included:

1) Social Service Agencies: Discussed their access to shelters, meal facilities, substance abuse programs, government benefit programs. And also the problems or overall satisfaction with services provided by public agencies was discussed.

2) Social Relations: Marital status, family relations and other interpersonal relations with friends, co-workers and staff at social service agencies (both past and present) were discussed. The intent is to establish the individual's social integration and also, to establish the type and usefulness of the assistance they receive from their interpersonal relations. We also discussed how often they are able to maintain social contact? How comfortable they feel asking for help? And overall, how they feel about the relationships they have in their lives.

3) Labor Market Integration: Their experiences with employment in the U.S. and if applicable in their country of origin (for recent immigrants) were discussed. Participants were asked about wages earned, occupation, unemployment rate and overall satisfaction with their job situation. When applicable, some Latino men were asked problems related to their undocumented work status (i.e., lack of legal work permits for immigrants that were illegally in the U.S.).

4) Migrant Experience: Recent immigrants were asked to discuss the characteristics of their migrant experience. For example: their prior experiences in the U.S.; their family's prior U.S. experience; their immigration status (legal or illegal); and the migrant status of other members of their family. Overall, illustrating how these factors affect their social and economic integration in the U.S. and specifically, how this affects their social exchange relations.

Research Site Selection and Sampling Design

Homeless Latino and African American participants in this study were primarily recruited from the downtown Los Angeles Skid Row area and also partially from bordering areas in East Los Angeles. Downtown Los Angeles' Skid Row area represents one of the nation's major concentrations of inner-city homeless. Here an estimated 17,200 to 42,500 homeless individuals congregate for services (Shelter Partnership 1994). On a daily basis, L.A.'s Skid Row area provides over 1,000 beds and almost 5,000 meals to those in need (Farr 1984). The homeless population in Skid Row primarily consists of single, nonwhite, adult males and only 10% are women (Koegel, et. al. 1988;

Hamilton, et. al. 1987). The estimated population composition is as follows: 40% are African American; 25% are white; 25% are Latinos; and 5% are Native Americans (Koegel, et. al. 1988; Hamilton, et. al. 1987). To account for the diverse social integration of recent immigrants, as compared to native-born Latinos a comparable sample size for each subgroup was selected. Therefore, in order to obtain an adequate sample of homeless Latinos, it was necessary to recruit Latino participants from or near the East Los Angeles area (a high density Latino area of L.A.).

The complete sample of homeless Latinos and African Americans was taken at three locations: 1) meal facilities; 2) bed shelters; and 3) outdoors on the streets of Skid Row or neighboring areas of Olvera Street (a Latino oriented tourist attraction near downtown) and a shelter in East Los Angeles. It was important to draw a sample from each location because homeless individuals making use of specific services or choosing to sleep out on the streets may have very distinct network connections and preferences.

For each of the three sampling sectors, the bed sector, the meal sector and the street sector, prospective homeless participants were screened to see if: 1) they met the 'homeless criteria' set by this study; 2) they were at least 18 years of age; 3) they were recent immigrants (5 years or less in U.S.A.), native-born Latinos, or long-term U.S. residents (more than 5 years in the U.S.); and 4) they were already screened or interviewed by this research project. The point was to maintain an unduplicated and random sample of homeless individuals for each sector. Other studies have also attempted to maintain an exclusive sample of each sector, that is, with no cross-over between those using bed facilities, meal facilities or those opting against the use of either of these services and prefer to sleep out on the street (Koegel et al., 1988; Farr 1984).

However, my interest is in understanding the process through which homeless persons initiate, access and maintain supportive social networks in gaining the resources they require for daily survival and their perceptions about the benefits and liabilities generated by these networks. This means then, that data on their use of several institutional services (bed and meal facilities), as well as their access to interpersonal support networks is an important contribution to my analysis.

QUALITATIVE DATA ANALYSIS AND CODING PROCEDURES

Qualitative research is by nature an inductive methodology that requires extensive analysis of the data, in order to formulate relevant theories regarding the phenomena in question. As the analysis progresses categories and patterns emerge that generate new hypotheses, which then help to further direct the on-going process of data evaluation. Ultimately, this analytical process culminates in the formulation of grounded theory (Glaser and Strauss, 1967; Glaser, 1978). The grounded theory approach to qualitative research emphasizes discovery and theory development, which proceed simultaneously and rest on an analytically inductive strategy for data evaluation (Charmaz, 1983). Grounded theorists are not so much adhering to an atheoretical orientation, rather their efforts are geared toward examination of the processes that are fundamental in ongoing social life, this is for them the point at which theoretical construction begins (Charmaz, 1983).

Grounded theorists generate theory in two ways: 1) through constant data comparison that yield conceptual categories and properties; and 2) using theoretical sampling, new data are collected in order to elaborate on rather than verify a particular theory (Charmaz, 1983). Glaser explains that:

> While in the field, the researcher continually asks questions as to fit, relevance and workability about the emerging categories and relationships between them [edited] . . . he continually fits his analysis to the data by checking as he proceeds. (1978:39)

In general I find the analytical framework of grounded theory a useful methodology. However, I am not convinced that researchers are completely free of apriori assumptions about social processes under study. Therefore, the application of grounded theory in this work involves the use of preliminary concepts and categories that were refined as the data analysis progressed.

Initially the analysis of qualitative data involved a process of categorizing and sorting data. After extensive data analysis conceptual categories become apparent. Although I did begin with a general social network framework, highlighting the network characteristics, the data actually served to refine and in some instances completely redefine some preliminary categories. However, in order to begin to generate conceptualizations of the social network process, the social relations of members, and the saliency of network participation for homeless members—the data search and sorting process was carried out with the following network characteristics in mind:

Attributes of Networks

1) Informal Networks: network membership involving informal ties with either friends, associates and/or casual acquaintances.
2) Type and Flow of Network Resources: resources or support generated by the network, either material or expressive in nature (e.g., moral support & companionship).

3) Density: The extent to which members of the network know and socialize with each other (ratio of actual ties to all possible ties).

Attributes of Links

1) Relationships: types of relationships existing within the network (e.g., casual acquaintances, associates or friends). Also examined here, is the social context through which the relationship was established (e.g., school friends, co-workers, street buddies).
2) Mode and Frequency of Contact: Method of contact employed to communicate with network members (e.g., face to face, phone, mail correspondence), and how often contact is established.
3) Closeness: emotional intimacy and personal attachments existing among network members. 4) Reciprocity: the extent to which network members mutually support each other (emotionally or materially) or extent of unidirectional support (lack of reciprocity).

Saliency of Network Ties

1) Network Benefits and Liabilities: participant's assessments of the utility of network involvement (their likes and dislikes regarding membership). Perceived benefits and costs involved in participating in personal and/or social networking.
2) Saliency and Purposive Nature of Relationships: Member's personal assessments of the meaning, purpose and social intimacy existing in their ties to network members.

Bibliography

Andrade, Sally Jones. *Living in the Gray Zone: Health Care Needs of Homeless Persons*. Austin, Texas: Benedictine Health Resource Center, 1988.

Arce, Anthony, Marilyn Tadlock, Michael J. Vergare. "A Psychiatric Profile of Street People Admitted to an Emergency Shelter." *Hospital and Community Psychiatry* 34 (1983): 812–17.

Appelbaum, Richard P. "The Affordability Gap." *Society* 26, no.4 (1989): 6–8.

Auslander, Gail K. and Howard Litwin. *Social Networks and the Poor: Toward Effective Policy and Practice*. National Association of Social Workers, Inc, 1988.

Bahr, Howard. (1967). The Gradual Disappearance of Skid Row. *Social Problems* 15 (1967): 41–45.

Bahr, Howard. "Homelessness, Disaffiliation, and Retreatism." In *Disaffiliation Man*, edited by Howard Bahr. Toronto: University of Toronto Press, 1970.

Bahr, Howard. *Skid Row: An Introduction to Disaffiliation*. New York: Oxford University Press, 1973.

Bahr, Howard and Theodore Caplow. *Old Men Drunk and Sober*. New York: New York University Press, 1973.

Baker, Susan G. "Gender, Ethnicity, and Homelessness: Accounting for Demographic Diversity on the Streets." *American Behavioral Scientist* 37, no.4 (1994): 476–504.

Bao, Wan-Ning, Les B. Whitbeck and Dan R. Hoyt. "Abuse, Support, and Depression among Homeless and Runaway Adolescents." *Journal of Health and Social Behavior* 41 (2000): 408–420.

Barak, Gregg. *Gimme Shelter: A Social History of Homelessness in Contemporary America*. Westport, CT: Praeger, 1992.

Bean, Frank., Jennifer Van Hook and Karen Woodrow-Lafield. *Estimates of Numbers of Unauthorized Migrants Residing in the United States: The Total, Mexican, and Non-Mexican Central American Unauthorized Populations in Mid2002*. Washington, D. C: Pew Hispanic Center, 2002.

Belcher, John and Frederick DiBlasio. 1990 *Helping the Homeless: Where Do We Go From Here?* Lexington, Massachusetts, Toronto: Lexington Books, D. C. Heath & Company, 1990.

Bell, Wendell and Marion Boat. "Urban Neighborhoods and Informal Social Relations." *American Journal of Sociology* 62 (January 1957): 391–398.

Bellah, Robert, Richard Madsen, William Sullivan, Ann Swidler and Steven Tipton. *Habits of the Heart: Individualism and Commitment in American Life.* New York: Oxford University Press, 1985.

Bhaskar, Roy. *The Possibility of Naturalism.* Brighton: Harvester, 1979.

Bingham, Richard D., Roy E. Green and Sammis B. White. *The Homeless in Contemporary Society.* Newbury PK., CA: Sage Publications, 1987.

Bittner, Egon. "The Police on Skid Row: A Study of Police Keeping." *American Sociology Review* 32 (1967): 699–715.

Blau, Joel. *The Visible Poor: Homelessness in America.* New York: Oxford University Press, 1992.

Blazer, Dan G. "Impact of Late-Life Depression on the Social Network." *American Journal of Psychiatry* 140 (1983): 162–165.

Blumberg, Leonard. Thomas Shipley and Joseph O. Moor. "The Skid Row Man and the Skid Row Status Community". *Quarterly Journal of Studies on Alcohol* 32 (1971): 909–941.

Blumer, Herbert. *Symbolic Interactionism: Perspective and Method.* Englewood Cliffs, N. J.: Prentice Hall, 1969.

Bogard, Cynthia J., Jeff J. McConnell, Naomi Gerstel and Michael Schwartz. "Homeless Mothers and depression: Misdirected policy." *Journal of Health and Social Behavior* 40 (1999): 46–62.

Boissevain, Jeremy and J. Clyde Mitchell. *Network Analysis: Studies in Human Interaction.* The Hague: Mouton, 1973.

Borjas, George J. and Marta Tienda. *Hispanics in the U.S. Economy.* Orlando, FL: Academic Press, Inc, 1985.

Boyd, Monica. "Family and Personal Networks in International Migration: Recent Developments and New Agendas." *International Migration Review* 23 (1989): 638–670.

Browning, Harley L. and Nestor Rodriquez. "The Migration of Mexican Indocumentados as a Settlement Process: Implications for Work." Pp. 277–297 in *Hispanics in the U.S. Economy*, edited by G. Borjas and M. Tienda. FL: Academic Press, 1985.

Bruner, Ed M. "Kin and Non-Kin." In *Urban Anthropology*, edited by A. Southall. New York: Oxford University Press, 1973.

Burns, Patrick, Dan Flaming, and Brent Haydamack. "Homeless in LA." Economic Roundtable. 2003. http://bringlahome.org/reports/htm (November 2003).

Burt, Martha. *Over the Edge: The Growth of Homelessness in the 1980's.* New York: Russell Sage Foundation, 1992.

Burt, Martha, Landon Aron, Edgar Lee and Jesse Valente. *Helping America's Homeless: Emergency Shelter or Affordable Housing?* Washington, D. C.: Urban Institute Press, 2001.

Burton, C. Emory. *The Poverty Debate: Politics and the Poor in America.* Westport, Conneticut: Praeger, 1992.

Cambell, Karen E., Peter V. Marsden and Jeanne S. Hurlburt. "Social Resources and Socioeconomic Status." *Social Networks* 8 (1986): 97–117.

Caplow, Theodore. "The Sociologist and the Homeless Man." In *Disaffiliated Man,* edited by H. Bahr. Toronto: University of Toronto Press, 1940.

Charmaz, Kathy. "The Grounded Theory Method." Pp. 109–126 in *Contemporary Field Research: A Collection of Readings,* edited by Robert Emerson. Prospect Heights, IL.: Waveland Press, 1988.

Chavez, Leo R. *Shadowed Lives: Undocumented Immigrants in American Society.* Forth Worth, Texas: Harcourt Brace Jovanovich, 1992.

Choldin, Harvey M. "Kinship Networks in the Migration Process." *International Migration Review* 7 (1973): 163–175.

Chudacoff, Howard P. *The Evolution of American Urban Society.* Englewood Cliffs, NJ: Prentice Hall, 1975.

Coates, Robert C. *A Street is Not a Home: Solving America's Homeless Dilemna.* Buffalo, New York: Prometheus Books, 1990.

Cohen, Carl and Jay Sokolovsky. *Old Men of the Bowery:Strategies for Survival Among the Homeless.* New York, London: The Guilford Press, 1989.

Conley, Dalton C. "Getting It Together: Social and Institutional Obstacles to Getting off the Streets." *Sociological Forum* 11, no.1 (March 1996): 25–40.

Cook, Karen. "Network Structures from an Exchange Perspective." Paper presented at the conference on Contributions of Network Analysis to Structural Sociology, Albany, NY, 1981.

Cousineau, Michael and Thomas Ward. *An Evaluation of the 1990 Census of the Homeless in Los Angeles.* The Los Angeles Homeless Health Care Project, Census Evaluation 1 (June 8, 1990).

Cousineau, Michael. "Comparing Adults in Los Angeles County Who Have And Have Not Been Homeless." *Journal of Community Psychology* 29, no. 6 (2001).

Craven, Paul and Barry Wellman. "The Network City." *Sociological Inquiry* 43 (1973): 57–88.

Crystal, Steven, Mervyn Goldstein, and Rosanne Levitt. *Chronic and Situational Dependency: Long-Term Residents in a Shelter for Men.* New York: Human Resources Administration, 1982.

Davis, James. "Clustering and Hierarchy in Interpersonal Relations." *Sociological Review* 35 (1970): 843–852.

DeNavas-Walt, Carmen, Bernadette D. Proctor, and Cheryl Hill Lee. "Income, Poverty and Health Insurance Coverage in the United States: 2004." Washington, D.C.: U.S. Census Bureau, Current Population Reports (2005): P60–229.

Eckenrode, John. "The Mobilization of Social Supports: Some Individual Constraints." *American Journal of Community Psychology* 11 (1983): 509–528.

Elliott, Marta and Lauren J. Krivo. "Structural Determinants of Homelessness in the United States." *Social Problems* 38, no. 1 (February 1991).

Ellwood, David T. *Poor Support: Poverty in the American Family.* New York: Basic Books, 1988.

Emirbayer, Mustafa and Jeff Goodwin. "Network Analysis, Culture and the Problem of Agency." *American Journal of Sociology* 99 (1994): 1411–54.

Farr, Rodger K. "The Los Angeles Skid Row Mental Health Project." *Psychosocial Rehabilitation Journal* 8 (1984): 64–76.

Fields, Jason. "America's Families and Living Arrangements: 2003." Washington, D.C.: U.S. Census Bureau, Current Population Reports, P20–553 (November 2004).

Fischer, Claude S. "Urbanism as a Way of Life: A Review and an Agenda." *Sociological Methods and Research* 1 (November 1972): 187–242.

Fischer, Claude S., Robert M. Jackson, C A. Stueve, Kathleen Gerson, Lynn McCallister-Jones and M ark Baldassare. *Networks and Places: Social Relations in the Urban Setting.* New York: The Free Press, Collier Macmillan Publishers, 1977.

Fischer, Claude S. *To Dwell Among Friends.* Berkeley: University of California Press, 1982.

Freeman, Richard B. and Brian Hall. *Permanent Homelessness in America.* Working Paper no.13. Cambridge, Mass: National Bureau of Economic Research, 1986.

Frey, Frederick, Elias Abrutyn, David Metzger, Georg Woody, Charles O'Brien and Paul Trusiani. "Focal Networks and HIV Risk among African-Male Intravenous Drug Users." Pp. 89–108, NIDA Research Monograph, No. 151 in *Social Networks, Drug Abuse and HIV Transmission*, edited by R. Needle and R. Trotter. Rockville, MD: National Institute on Drug Abuse, 1995.

Garret, Gerald R. and Russell K. Schutt. "Homelessness in Massachusetts: Description and Analysis." Pp. 57–72, v. 1 in *Homelessness in the United States: State Surveys*, edited by Jamshid A. Momeni. Westport, Conn.: Greenwood Press, Inc., 1989.

Geertz, Clifford. "Thick Description: Toward an Interpretive Theory of Culture." Pp. 37–59 in *Contemporary Field Research: A Collection of Readings*, edited by Robert Emerson. Prospect Heights, IL.: Waveland Press, 1988.

Giddens, Anthony. *The Constitution of Society.* Cambridge, England: Polity Press, 1984.

Glaser, Barney. *Theoretical Sensitivity.* Mill Valley, CA: Sociology Press, 1978.

Glaser, Barney and Anselm Strauss. *The Discovery of Grounded Theory: Strategies for Qualitative Research.* Chicago: Aldine, 1967.

Gottlieb, Benjamin. "Preventive Interventions Involving Social Networks and Social Support." In *Social Networks and Social Support*, edited by B. Gottlieb. Beverly Hills, CA: Sage Publications, Inc, 1981.

Gouldner, Alvin. *For Sociology.* London: Allen Lane, 1973.

Granovetter, Mark S. "The Strength of Weak Ties." *American Journal of Sociology* 78 (1973): 1360–1380.

Greenstein, Robert and Art Jaeger. *Number in Poverty Hits 20–year High as Recession Adds 2 Million More Poor, Analysis Finds.* Washington, D.C.: Center in Budget and Policy Priorities, 1992.

Griffith, James. "Social Support Providers: Who Are They? Where Are They Met? And the Relationship of Network Characteristics to Psychological Distress." *Basic and Applied Social Psychology* 6 (1985): 41–60.

Grigsby, Charles, Donald Bauman, Steven Gregorish and Cynthia Roberts-Gray. "Disaffiliation to Entrenchment: A Model for Understanding Homelessness." *Journal of Social Issues* 46 (1990): 141–156.

Hamilton, Rabinowitz, and Alschuler. *The Changing Face of Misery: Los Angeles' Skid Row Area in Transition, Housing and Social Service Needs of Central City East.* Los Angeles: Community Redevelopment Agency, 1987.

Heskin, Allen. "Los Angeles Innovative Local Approaches." In *The Homeless in Contemporary Society,* edited by Bingham, R., R. Green and S. White. Los Angeles: Sage Publication, 1987.

Hirsch, Barton J. "Social Networks and the Coping Process: Creating Personal Communities." In *Social Networks and Social Support,* edited by Benjamin Gottlieb. Beverly Hills, CA: Sage Publications, Inc, 1981.

Hoch, Charles and Robert Slayton. *New Homeless and Old: Community and the Skid Row Hotel.* Philadelphia: Temple University Press, 1989.

Hombs, Mary Ellen and Mitch Synder. *Homelessness in America: A Forced March to Nowhere.* Washington, D.C.: Community for Creative Non-Violence, 1982.

Hurlbert, Jeanne, Valerie Haines and John Beggs. "Core Networks and Tie Activation: What Kinds of Routine Networks Allocate Resources in Non-routine Situations?" *American Sociological Review* 65 (2000): 598–618.

Jackson, Max. "Social Structure and Process in Friendship Choice." In *Network and Places: Social Relations in the Urban Setting,* edited by Claude Fischer. New York: The Free Press, Collier Macmillan Publishers, 1977.

Jencks, Christopher. *The Homeless.* Cambridge, Massachusetts: Harvard University Press, 1994.

Jensen, Lief. "Poverty and Immigration in the United States: 1960–1980." Pp. 117–136 in *Divided Opportunities,* edited by Sandefur and Tienda. New York: Plenum Press, 1988.

Johnson, Kurt, Les B. Whitbeck, Dan R. Hoyt. "Predictors of social network composition among homeless and runaway adolescents." *Journal of Adolescence* 28 (2005): 231–248.

Kasarda, John. "Urban Change and Minority Opportunities." In *The New Urban Reality,* edited by Peterson. Washington, D. C.: Brookings Institute, 1985.

Katz, Fred. "Occupational Contact Networks." *Social Forces* 37, no. 1 (1966): 52–55.

Katz, Jack. "A Theory of Qualitative Methodology: The Social System of Analytic Fieldwork." Pp. 127–148 in *Contemporary Field Research: A Collection of Readings,* edited by Robert Emerson. Prospect Heights, IL.: Waveland Press, 1988.

Koegel, Paul, and Audrey Burnam. "Traditional and Nontraditional Alcoholics." *Alcohol Health and Research World* 11, no. 3 (Spring 1987).

Koegel, Paul, Audrey Burnam and Rodger K. Farr. "The Prevalence of Specific Psychiatric Disorders Among Homeless Individuals in the Inner City of Los Angeles." *Archives of General Psychiatry* 45 (1988): 1085–1092.

Koegel, Paul, Elan Melamid, and Audrey Burnam. "Childhood Risk Factors for Homelessness among Homeless Adults." *American Journal of Public Health* 85, no.12 (1995): 1642–1649.

Kozol, Jonathan. *Rachel and Her Children: Homeless Families in America.* New York: Crown, 1988.

La Gory, Mark, Ferris J. Ritchey, Timothy O'Donoghue and Jeffrey Mullis. "Homelessness in Alabama: A Variety of People and Experiences." In *Homelessness in the United States: State Surveys, 1,* 1–20, edited by Jamshid A. Momeni. Westport, Conn.: Greenwood Press, Inc, 1989.

Lazarfeld, Paul and Robert Merton. "Friendship as Social Process." In *Freedom and Control in American,* edited by M. Berger et al.. New York: Van Nostrand, 1954.

Lazarus, Emma. "The New Colossus." Sonnet engraved on plaque mounted inside the Statue of Liberty, 1883.

Lin, Nan. "Building a network theory of social capital." Pp. 3–30 in *Social Capital: Theory and Research,* edited by Nan Lin, K. Cook, and R.S.B. Hawthrone. New York: Aldine de Gruyter, 2001.

Lofland, John and Lyn Lofland. *Analyzing Social Settings: A Guide to Qualitative Observation and Analysis.* Belmont, CA: Wadsworth, 1995

Los Angeles Community Redevelopment Agency. *Public Policy in Central City East:1974–1985.* Los Angeles. December. p.1, 1985.

Los Angeles Homeless Service Authority. "Continuum of Care Narrative for Super NOFA 2003 Application." http://lahsa.org/continuum.htm (2003).

Lovell, Anne. "Marginality Without Isolation: Social Networks and the New Homeless." Paper presented at the 83rd Annual Meeting of the American Anthropological Association. Denver, Colorado, 1984.

Lowell, Lindsay. and Roberto Suro. *How Many Undocumented: The numbers behind the U.S.—Mexico Migration Talks.* Washington, D.C.: The Pew Hispanic Center, 2002.

MacDonald, John S. and Leatrice D. MacDonald. (1974). "Chain Migration, Ethnic Neighborhood Formation, and Social Networks." Pp. 226–235 in *An Urban World,* edited by C. Tillly. Boston: Little, Brown, 1974.

MacKnee, Chuck and Jennifer Mervyn. "Critical Incidents that Facilitate Homeless People's Transition Off the Streets." *Journal of Social Distress and the Homeless* 11, no.4 (2002): 293–306.

Maram, Sheldon L. (1980). "Hispanic Workers in the Garment and Restaurant Industries in Los Angeles County". Working Papers in U.S.-Mexican Studies, No. 12. La Jolla, CA. University of California, San Diego: Center for U.S.—Mexican Studies, 1980.

Marcelli, Enerico, Manuel Pastor and Pascale M Joassart. (1999). "Estimating the effects of informal Economic Activity: Evidence from Los Angeles County." *Journal of Economic Issues* 33, no. 3 (1999): 579–607.

Marcuse, Peter. (1988). "Gentrification, Abandonment, and Displacement: Connection, Causes, and Policy Response in New York City." *Washington University Journal of Urban and Contemporary Law* 28 (1988): 195–240.

Massey, Douglas, Rafael Alarcon, Jorge Durand and Humberto Gonzalez. *Return to Aztlan: The Social Process of International Migration from Western Mexico.* Berkeley and Los Angeles, CA: University of California Press, Ltd., 1987.

McCarthy, Kevin F. and Burciaga R. Valdez. *Current and Future Effects of Mexican Immigration in California.* R-3365–CR. Santa Monica, CA: The Rand Corporation. 1986.

McCarty, Christopher. "Measuring Structure in Personal Networks." Journal of Social Structure 3, no. 1 (2002).

McFate, Katherine, Roger Lawson and William J. Wilson. *Poverty, Inequality and the Future of Social Policy: Western States in the New World Order.* New York: Russell Sage Foundation, 1995.

McGeary, Michael and Lynn Laurence. *Urban Change and Poverty.* Washington, D.C.: National Academy Press, 1988.

McKinney-Vento Homeless Assistance Act. http://www.hud.gov/offices/cpd/homeless/library/esg/esgdeskguide/section4.cfm (1987 & 2002)

McKinnon, Jesse. (2003). "The Black Population in the United States: March 2002." Washington D.C.: U.S. Census Bureau, Current Population Reports, Series P. 20–541, 2002.

Mercier, Celine and Guylaine Racine. "A Follow-up Study of Homeless Women." *Journal of Social Distress and the Homeless* 2 (1993): 207–221.

Merton, Robert K. *Social Theory and Social Structure.* Glencoe: Free Press, 1949

Mindel, Charles H. (1980). "Extended Familialism Among Urban Mexican Americans, Anglos and Blacks." *Hispanic Journal of Behavior Sciences* 2 (1980): 21–34.

Mindel, Charles and R. Wright. "The Use of Social Services by Black and White Elderly: The Role of Social Support Systems." *Journal of Gerontological Social Work* 4 (1982): 107–125.

Mitchell, J. Clyde. "The Components of Strong Ties Among Homeless Women. Social Networks." 3 (1987): 37–47.

Mitchel, Robert E. "Some Social Implications of High Density Housing." *American Sociological Review* 36 (February 1971): 18–29.

Molina, Edna. "Informal Non-kin Networks among Homeless Latino and African American Men: Form and Functions." *American Behavioral Scientist* 43, no. 4 (2000): 663–685.

Morse, Gary, N. Shields, Christine Hanneke, Robert Calsyn, Gary Burger, and Bruce Nelson. *Homeless People in St. Louis: A Mental Health Program Evaluation.* Jefferson City, MO. Department of Mental Health, 1985.

National Housing Institute. *Shelterforce.* November, December p.5, 1992.

O'Flaherty, Brendon. *Making Room: The Economics of Homelessness.* Cambridge, MA: Harvard University Press, 1996.

Oliver, Melvin. "The Urban Black Community as Network: Toward a Social Network Perspective." *Sociological Quarterly* 29, no. 4 (1988): 623–645.

Pittman, David J. and C. Wayne Gordon. *Revolving Door: A Study of the Chronic Police Case Inebriate.* Glencoe: Free Press, 1958.

Portes, Alejandro and Robert L. Bach. *Latin Journey: Cuban and Mexican Immigrants in the United States.* Berkeley and Los Angeles, CA: University of California Press, Ltd., 1985.

Portes, Alejandro and Joszef Borocz. "Contemporary Immigration: Theoretical Perspectives on its Determinants and Modes of Incorporation." *International Migration Review* 23 (1989): 606–630.

Ramirez, Roberto R., and G. Patricia de la Cruz. "The Hispanic Population in the United Status: March 2002." Washington, D. C.: U. S. Census Bureau, Current Population Reports, P20–545. 2002.

Redburn, Stevens F. and Terry Buss. *Responding to America's Homeless.* New York, N.Y.: Praeger Publishers, 1986.

Rooney, James. "Group Processes Among Skid Row Winos: A Reevaluation of the Under-socialized Hypothesis." *Quarterly Journal of Studies on Alcohol* 22 (1961): 444–460.

Rooney, James. "Friendship and Disaffiliation Among the Skid Row Population." *Journal of Gerontology* 31 (1976): 82–88.

Ropers, Richard H. *The Invisible Homeless.* New York: Insight Books, 1988.

Rosenthal, Robert. *Homeless in Paradise: A Map of the Terrain.* Philadelphia: Temple University Press, 1994.

Rossi, Peter., James Wright, G. A. Fischer and G. Willis. "The Urban Homeless." *Science* 235 (1987): 1336–1341.

Rossi, Peter H. "Minorities and Homelessness." In *Divided Opportunities:Minorities, Poverty, and Social Policy,* edited by Gary D. Sandefur and Marta Tienda. New York: Plenum Press, 1988.

Rossi, Peter H. *Down and Out in America.* Chicago: University of Chicago Press, 1989.

Roth, Dee and G. Jerry Bean. *Alcohol Problems and Homelessness: Findings from the Ohio Study.* Ohio Department of Mental Health, Office of Program Evaluation and Research. July 1985.

Roth, Dee and G. Jerry Bean. *New Perspectives on Homelessness: Findings from a Statewide Epidemiological Study.* Hospital and Community Psychiatry, 1986.

Rubin, Zick. *Liking and Loving.* New York: Holt, Rinehart and Winston, 1973.

Sewell, William. "A Theory of Structure: Duality, Agency, and Transformation." *American Journal of Sociology* 98 (1992): 1–29.

Shapiro, Joan. *Communities of the Alone.* New York: Association Press, 1971.

Shelter Partnership. "The Number of Homeless People Nightly in Los Angeles County, July 1980 to June 1990," p.ii. December 1990.

Shelter Partnership. "The Number of Homeless People in Los Angeles City and County, July 1993 to June 1994." 1995.

Shinn, Marybeth and Colleen Gillespie. "The Roles of Housing and Poverty in the Origins of Homelessness." *American Behavioral Scientist* 37 (February 1994): 505–521.

Smith, Annetta and Denise Smith. U.S. Census Bureau, Census Special Reports, Series CENSR/01–2, *Emergency and Transitional Shelter Populations: 2000.* Washington D.C.: U.S. Government Printing Office, 2001.

Snow, David, Susan Gonzalez-Baker, Leon Anderson, and M. Martin. "The Myth of Pervasive Mental Illness Among the Homeless." *Social Problems* 33 (1986): 407–423.

Snow, David and Leon Anderson. "Identity Work Among the Homeless: The Verbal Construction and Avowal of Personal Identities." *American Journal of Sociology* 92, no. 6 (1987): 1365–1371.

Snow, David A. and Leon Anderson. *Down on Their Luck: A Study of Homeless Street People*. Berkeley: University of California Press, 1992.

Sosin, Michael. "Homeless and Vulnerable Program Users." *Social Problems* 39 (1992): 170–188.

Sosin, Michael, Paul Colson and Susan Grossman. *Homelessness in Chicago: Poverty and Pathology, Social Institutions and Social Change*. Chicago: Chicago Community Trust, 1988.

Stack, Carol B. (1974). *All Our Kin*. New York: Harper and Row, 1974.

Stark, Louisa. "The Shelter as 'Total Institution,' An Organizational Barrier to Remedying Homelessness." *American Behavioral Scientist* 37(February 1994): 553–562.

State of California Interagency Task Force on Homelessness. "A Summary Report on California's Programs to Address Homelessness." March 2002.

Strauss, Robert. "Alcohol and the Homeless Man." *Quarterly Journal of Studies on Alcohol* 7 (1946): 360–404.

Timmer, Doug A., D. Stanley Eitzen, and Kathryn D. Talley. *Paths to Homelessness: Extreme Poverty and the Urban Housing Crisis*. Boulder, Colorado: Westview Press, 1994.

Toohey, Siobhan, Marybeth Shinn, and Beth Weitzman. "Social Networks and Homelessness Among Women Heads of Household." *American Journal of Community Psychology* 33, nos. 1&2 (2004): 7–20.

United States Bureau of the Census. "The Black Population in the United States: March 1990 and 1989." Current Population Reports, Series P-20, no. 448. Washington, DC: U.S. Government Printing Office, 1991.

United States Bureau of the Census. "The Hispanic Population in the United States: March 1990." Current Population Reports, Series P-20, no. 449. Washington, D.C.: U.S. Government Printing Office, 1990.

United States Bureau of the Census. "American Fact Finder: United States 2004 American Community Survey Data Profile Highlights." *http://factfinder.census.gov* (2004).

United States Bureau of the Census. "Facts for Features: Hispanic Heritage Month 2005: September 15–October 15." http://www.census.gov/Press-release/www/releases/archives/population/005514.htm (2005).

United States Conference of Mayors, Hunger and Homelessness Survey. "A Status Report on Hunger and Homelessness in America's Cities, A 25–City Survey." December 2004.

United States Department of Commerce News. "S-Night Operations." P. 1 March 20–21, 1990.

United States Department of Commerce News. "Census Bureau Releases, 1990 Decennial Counts of Persons Enumerated in Emergency Shelters and Observed on Streets" P. 2, December 1990–1991.

United States Department of Housing and Urban Development (HUD). "Helping the Homeless: A Resource Guide." Washington, D. C.: Office of Policy Development and Research, 1984.

United States Department of Housing and Urban Development (HUD). "A report to the secretary on the homeless and emergency shelters." Washington, D.C.: Office of Public Development and Research, 1984.

United States Department of Housing and Urban Development. ESG Deskguide, Section 4.4, http://www.hud.gov/offices/cpd/homeless/library/esg/esgdeskguide/section4.cfm.

Urban Institute. http://www.urban.org/UploadedPDF/end_homelessness.pdf (2001).

Valentine, Bettylou. *Hustling and Other Hard Work: Life Styles in the Ghetto.* New York: Free Press, 1978.

Wagner, David. *Checkerboard Square: Culture and Resistance in a Homeless Community.* Boulder, Colorado: Westview Press, Inc., 1993

Waldinger, Roger. "Network, bureaucracy, and exclusion: Recruitment and selection in an immigrant metropolis." Pp. 228–259 in *Immigration and opportunity: Race, ethnicity, and employment in the United States,* edited by F. Bean and S. Bell-Rose. New York: Russell Sage Foundation, 1999.

Wallace, Samuel. *Skid Row as a Way of Life.* Totawa, NJ: Bedminister, 1965.

Warren, Donald I. "Using Helping Networks: A Key Social Bond of Urbanitites." In *Community Support Systems in Mental Health,* edited by D. Biegel and A. Naparstek. New York: Springer Publishing Co, 1982.

Warren, Robert and Jeffrey S. Passel. " A Count of the Uncountable: Estimates of Undocumented Aliens Counted in the 1980 Census." Unpublished paper, 1984.

Wasserman, Stanely and Katherine Faust. *Social Network Analysis: Methods and Applications.* Cambridge, MA: Cambridge University Press, 1994.

Weber, Max. *Wirtschaft und Gesellschaft.* Translated as, *Economy and Society: An Outline of Interpretive Sociology.* New York: Bedminster Press, 1922.

Weitzman, Beth C., James R. Knickman and Marybeth Shinn. "Pathways to homelessness among New York City families." *Journal of Social Issues* 46 (1990): 125–140.

Wellman, Barry. *Network Analysis: Some Basic Principles.* Sociological Theory. San Francisco: Jossey-Bass, 1983.

Wellman, Barry. "Which Types of Ties and Networks Provide Which Type of Social Support?" *Advances in Group Processes* 9 (1992): 207–235.

Wilson, William Julius. *The Truly Disadvantaged.* Chicago and London. University of Chicago Press, 1987.

Wilson, William Julius. *When Work Disappears: The World of the New Urban Poor.* New York: Alfred A. Knopf, Inc., 1996.

Wiseman, Jacqueline. *Stations of the Lost.* Chicago: University of Chicago Press, 1970.

Wolf, Eric R. "Kinship, Friendship, and Patron-Client Relations." In *Social Anthropology of Complex Societies,* edited by M. Banton. London: Tavistock: ASA Monograph, no. 4, 1966.

Wong, Yin Ling Irene and Irving Pilivan. "A dynamic analysis of homeless-domicile transitions." *Social Problems* 44, no. 3 (1997): 408–423.

Wright, James D. and E. Weber. *Homelessness and Health*. New York: Mc Graw Hill, 1987.

Wright, James D. *Address Unknown: The Homeless in America*. Hawthrone, New York: Walter de Gruyter, Inc., 1989.

Wright, James D., Beth Rubin and Joel Devine. *Beside the Golden Door: Policy, Politics and the Homeless*. Hawthorne, NY: Aldine de Gruyter, 1998.

Wright, Talmadge. *Out of Place: Homeless Mobilization, Subcities, and Contested Landscapes*. New York, Albany: State University of New York Press, 1997.

Wright, Talmadge. "Resisting Homelessness: Global, National and Local Solutions." *Contemporary Sociology* 29, no.1 (2000): 27–43. Utopian Visions: Engaged Sociologist for the 21st Century.

Yeich, Susan. *The Politics of Ending Homelessness*. Lanham, Maryland: University Press of America, Inc., 1994.

Index

acquaintances/associates of homeless men: acclamation to street life and, 66–67; casual acquaintances, 58–59, 61–62, 65; familiar strangers, 62–63; incidental meetings, 59–62; informational acquaintances, 60; personal freedom and, 64; as a protective mechanism, 63; saliency of weak ties, 57, 63, 108; social context of, 57–58. *See also* utilitarian link to associates

African American, family composition of, 22

African American homelessness: friendship linkages and, 82, 90, 92–93; versus Latino homelessness, 17–18, 46–53, 84, 85–86; non-kin networks and, 47–53; research on, 2; resource exchange capacity, 97, 99; role expectations and gender, 98, 99–100; social networking, 28–30; utilitarian link to associates, 66

African American labor force participation rate (male), 21

African American poverty, 22

African Americans, educational attainment of, 21

African Americans, U. S. population characteristics for, 21–22

age structure difference among African-Americans, white Americans, 21

agency, concept of, 11

aid to the poor as provisional, ix

Anderson and Snow (1993), 5, 41

Appelbaum, Richard P. (1989), viii, 123

asymmetrical power relations, 68–70, 99

Bahr, Howard (1967), 12, 123

Bahr, Howard (1973), 5, 123

Bahr, Howard and Theodore Caplow (1973), 19, 123

Bao, Wan-Ning et al. (2000), 1, 27, 40, 78, 111, 123

Barak, Gregg (1992), 11, 19, 123

Bean, Frank et al. (2002), 24, 123

Belcher, John and Frederick DiBlasio (1990), 25, 124

Bhaskar, Roy (1979), 12, 124

Bingham, Richard D., et al. (1987), 1, 124

Bitter, Egon (1967), 64, 124

Blau, Joel (1992), 20, 124

Blumer Herbert (1969), 11, 124

Bogard, Cynthia J., et al. (1999), 110, 124

Burns, Ed M., et al. (2003), 3, 124

About the Author

Edna Molina-Jackson is a professor of sociology specializing in the area of ethnic and racial stratification at the California State University, Bakersfield. She has authored articles on homelessness involving Latinos and African Americans, served as a reviewer on homelessness for the American Journal of Sociology and has worked as a consultant on a large-scale study on homelessness for the RAND Corporation (a non-profit research organization headquartered in Santa Monica, California). In addition, she has served on the editorial board of the journal, Gender and Society, and continues to serve as a reviewer for Sage Publication and other academic presses. Dr. Molina-Jackson earned her doctorate in sociology at the University of California, Los Angeles.